HOW TO DRINK
WHISKEY

HOW TO DRINK WHISKEY

13-Digit ISBN: 978-1-40034-059-0

10-Digit ISBN: 1-40034-059-4

This book may be ordered by mail from the publisher. Please include $5.99 for postage and handling.

Please support your local bookseller first!

Books published by Cider Mill Press Book Publishers are available at special discounts for bulk purchases in the United States by corporations, institutions, and other organizations. For more information, please contact the publisher.

Cider Mill Press Book Publishers
"Where good books are ready for press"
501 Nelson Place
Nashville, Tennessee 37214
cidermillpress.com

Typography: Knockout, Trade Gothic

Image Credits: Pages 15, 23, 27, 35, 42, 46, 81, 160, 167, 171, 173, 177, 178, 181, 184, 187, and 188 used under official license from Shutterstock. All other photos courtesy Carlo DeVito and Cider Mill Press.

Printed in the United States of America

24 25 26 27 28 VER 5 4 3 2 1
First Edition

HOW TO DRINK
WHISKEY

CARLO DEVITO

FROM GRAINS TO GLASSES,
EVERYTHING YOU NEED TO KNOW

CIDER MILL
PRESS

BOOK
PUBLISHERS

DEDICATION

To my father, Philip DeVito, who tried to teach me about elegant drinking (but who was a teetotaler at home).

And to the many men and women who shared their knowledge with me along the way.

And to our New England Craft Beverage Research Team: Richard Srsich, Dan Kirkhaus, and John Crabtree, who assisted in the research of whiskey in the name of knowledge.

CONTENTS

PROLOGUE

MIKE WILLIAMS'S
CHRISTMAS

What was Mike Williams's most memorable moment concerning Tennessee whiskey? His answer was instant and not what might be expected, especially since he is considered the father of modern Tennessee distilling: "When I came back from college after my freshman year, after my first semester. It was Christmas Eve, and my mother said it was time to go see Aunt Pauline and Uncle Claude. Which was the time the kids dreaded every year. We had to get in the car and go over to Claude and Pauline's house. And sit around in the living room and let them talk about how much we'd grown. And eat some fruitcake or something. And leave. It was just a wasted hour as far as we were concerned.

"This time I was back from college, and after we'd been there a few minutes, Uncle Claude said, 'Gentlemen, would you join me in the kitchen?' All the men got up . . . and then he turned around and looked at me, and said, 'You're a college man, come in the kitchen with us.' And Pauline said, 'Oh, Claude! Don't take him in there!' I hopped up and went off with the men into the kitchen. Claude poured everybody a shot of Jack Daniel's. He poured me a smaller shot. And he gave everybody a glass of water. Then he said, 'Gentlemen, Merry Christmas!' He tapped his glass two times on the counter. Everybody else tapped their shot glass two times on the counter. I tapped mine two times. We all threw them back and then took a drink of water. Everybody shook hands with each other. 'Merry Christmas! Let's have a great New Year.' And we went back to join the ladies in the living room.

"I didn't cough. I think my eyes might have run a little bit. They were probably a little bit blurry," Mike recalls. "It stung a little bit. And as I was walking out of the kitchen, back to the living room, Uncle Claude patted me on the back, and said, 'Well done, Mikey, well done.' That is my most memorable drink ever."

And that is what whiskey is all about.

INTRODUCTION

There is possibly nothing sexier or more suave about adulthood than going to a steakhouse or restaurant and having a few cocktails before the main attraction. People are usually well dressed, or at least coiffed. It's grown-up time.

I grew up a denizen of restaurants. Many of my father's friends were restaurateurs. We could never just walk in and sit down for dinner. You had to first say hello to at least three or four tables of people, and have at least one drink at the bar, whether they asked you to wait or not. More often, my father would, in his favorite restaurants, order his appetizers at the bar, and have them waiting for him at the table when he finally chose to sit down. This way he could hold forth at the bar a while and enjoy.

My father thoroughly enjoyed a cocktail or two before sitting down. To him, being at the bar was as much a part of the evening as the actual meal. Dressed in a jacket and tie, and always with a pocket square, he had no fear and could strike up a conversation with any stranger. He was not intimidated. On the contrary, he was convivial and chatty, and could hold forth on a number of topics. But his best attribute was getting people to talk about themselves. He would get people going on their favorite subject, and more often than not he was thoroughly entertained by what he learned from them. That was probably the best tip he gave to me about how to act at a bar: don't talk about yourself to someone else. The way to get them chatting is to have them tell you about themselves.

My father was not a drinker per se. Not the way I am. Despite the fact that we had literally a closet full of whiskey, vodka, gin, and a thousand cordials, my father rarely drank at home, and only when we had company. Sometimes, even when they indulged, he did not. There were thirty or forty bottles of whiskey alone. A vast array. Dewar's. Cutty Sark. J&B. McClelland's. Macallan. Pinch. Chivas Regal. Black & White. And so on. Gifts from clients and friends. During the week, my father drank coffee for breakfast with a bacon, egg, and cheese sandwich or a bagel with butter and cream cheese. Otherwise, he drank extremely weak iced tea (colored water, as we kids used to joke) or water with ice. That was it.

When I became a man with my own home and a family, the locations of our family gatherings began to subtly shift, as it does over the course of the lives of families. Since we were loaded down with small children and dogs, my parents slowly gave way, and our home became ground zero for holidays.

The first time my father came over, he asked what we had to drink. I looked at him quizzically. Water? Wine? Beer? He made a face.

No. He wanted a cocktail. I offered, vodka? Gin? It's what I had the most of at the time. It's what the zeitgeist of the cocktail world was then. He made a face. No!

I proffered bourbon. "Too sweet!" he scoffed. "Don't you have any good whiskey, kid? Scotch?" I shook my head.

"You gotta get some whiskey, kid!" he said with a sigh. From then on, I always had a bottle of single malt Scotch in the house whenever my father came to visit.

He seemed to have a ritual, as he always did with alcohol. He would be there for half an hour or so, and then turn, suddenly, no matter the situation, and say, "I think I could use a glass of whiskey."

The first time he did this, I poured a Tom Collins glass with three fingers of McClelland's Highland Single Malt. He looked at me in horror as I extended the brown liquid toward him.

"Don't you have any proper whiskey glasses?" he said with a smile. "Didn't I teach you anything? Gotta get some whiskey glasses. At least decent highball glasses."

He offered up his glass. "Add a splash of water. Just a drop." I placed it under the kitchen faucet, doused the whiskey, and handed the glass back to him. He made a face. As he took the glass, his eyebrows raised. "Jesus, don't drown it. Just a dab next time. A few drops. You want to let it breathe." He said it with a friendly tone, but as a son, I took it as admonishment.

"That's a lotta whiskey, kid!" he said, hoisting up the tall glass. "Not so much next time."

Later, I found a set of whiskey glasses he had bought me for my college graduation that had been buried away. Gold rimmed with ducks on the side in gold, as well. We shared many drinks in those glasses. That is another story.

Each time my father came over, another rule for enjoying whiskey was revealed. But after three or four years, I realized that each visit was a lesson in how to savor the spirit. He was trying to teach me something, life lessons I was usually averse to.

In time, I joined him, first sipping a bourbon next to his single malt. And then later the two of us enjoying our single malt Scotches together. We would stand on the front porch or the back deck, or sit by the fireplace watching the game, holding our drinks, and chatting. Talking about the Yankees, the Giants, politics, the news. He loved the news and was always up-to-date.

Yet another ritual in his life was born. And another passed down to me.

And every holiday, I made sure the bottle was full enough, or replaced it, so we would have enough for his next visit. It was his bottle. We moved over the years but no matter where I lived, no matter what house we celebrated in, I had his bottle at the ready. I look back on those moments as some of the best in my life.

About a year after he passed, I was cleaning out the liquor cabinet in our house, necessitated by yet another move. At the far back was the bottle I had kept for him. He had been sick before he had passed, and the bottle had gathered much dust in the meantime.

There was only a finger's worth left. I had been a bad son in letting it sit there, not having replaced it.

I poured the last dram in a proper glass, our gold-rimmed duck glasses, and put just a dab of water in it. And drank to him.

Someday it will be my turn to pass on these lessons. In the meantime, I drink to him. Because that, too, is what whiskey is all about.

HOW TO ORDER WHISKEY (OR WHISKY)

First up, the spelling. Generally speaking, the Scottish, Canadians, Australians, South Africans, New Zealanders, and Japanese spell it *whisky*. Americans and the Irish spell it *whiskey*. Of course, there are outliers.

No matter how you spell it, when you are ordering it at a bar or restaurant, there is terminology you need to be aware of:

NEAT: This means you want whiskey at room temperature without anything in it. The first time I have a whiskey I have never tasted before, I ask for it neat, so I can evaluate it. I'm not taking notes, except maybe mentally. But the idea is to appreciate the whiskey.

WATER BACK OR ON THE SIDE: You are asking the bartender to provide a glass of water on the side.

ICE BACK OR ON THE SIDE: You want a glass of ice on the side.

CUBE, ROCK, BALL, SPHERE OF ICE: When I have a choice, I prefer a large chunk of ice rather than smaller cubes. Why? Because it melts slower and, thus, dilutes the whiskey less.

ON THE ROCKS: The mixologist on duty will fill a whiskey glass with ice, then pour your whiskey in. Many people drink their whiskey this way. It dilutes the whiskey faster, and for those who are looking to nurse their drink, it isn't a bad decision.

WHISKEY WITH WATER: This is not a shot of water; it's just a small splash. It helps the whiskey aerate. It enhances the nose and dilutes the whiskey, usually killing off any burn the whiskey might have.

WITH A TWIST: Personally, I love almost any whiskey with either a lemon or orange peel, twisted in order to release the essential oils in the fruit's rind, adding fragrance and flavor.

UP: Used when ordering a classic whiskey cocktail—a Manhattan, Rob Roy, or Boulevardier—it means the drink will be shaken and strained into a coupe glass.

CHASER: When ordering a strong drink, like whiskey, some people prefer a milder beverage on the side, such as water, ginger ale or other soda, beer, or some other mixer.

TWO FINGERS OF WHISKEY: This means you want the level of whiskey in the glass to be the width of two fingers when you hold the glass. In some places, this is considered "a double."

JIGGER: A two-sided measuring unit. One side is marked for 1½ ounces, or a shot; and the other side is marked for ¾ ounce, which is a half shot.

WHAT TO DRINK YOUR WHISKEY IN

I used to think that the glass was not important, that the glassware industry was a lot of hype. I derided aficionados as dandies and dilettantes. I have a big mea culpa to swallow. The glass isn't everything, but it certainly helps. When tasting, you really do want a Glencairn glass or other tulip-shaped glass to funnel the nose upward. A whiskey or rocks glass is often a great utilitarian glass for whiskey on the rocks or a cocktail. A coupe glass is an indispensable cocktail necessity. And, of course, a Tom Collins glass is necessary for several versions of Whiskey and Soda (especially the Japanese Highball). Don't go crazy. You don't need a dozen different glasses, but having the right glass is a lot like wearing French cuffs and a nice set of links. It adds a little pizzazz to the experience, and it shows you're not a total buffoon.

SHOT GLASS: Usually just big enough to hold 1½ ounces, or a shot.

GLENCAIRN GLASS: This tulip-shaped glass is considered the best all-around glass to sip whiskey from. The small bowl at the bottom of the glass cradles the liquid, and the fluted top concentrates the aromas and funnels them toward the nose.

ROCKS GLASS: This is a cocktail glass. In drinking whiskey, it can serve whiskey neat or be used for whiskey on the rocks. It is usually eight to ten ounces. Perfect for whiskey pours.

DOUBLE ROCKS GLASS: This is generally two ounces larger than a rocks glass but it is not twice the size. It is sometimes referred to as a double old-fashioned glass.

HIGHBALL GLASS: Used for cocktails, especially a Highball (see page 189 for a recipe) or an Old Fashioned (see page 164). Usually about twelve ounces. Generally used with mixers.

TASTING VS. DRINKING

Whiskey is to grain as a diamond is to coal; it suffers an immense, intense crucible and comes out at the other end a sparkling, shiny thing to be marveled at. Making whiskey is an alchemist's art.

When I am drinking a good whiskey for the first time, I order the whiskey

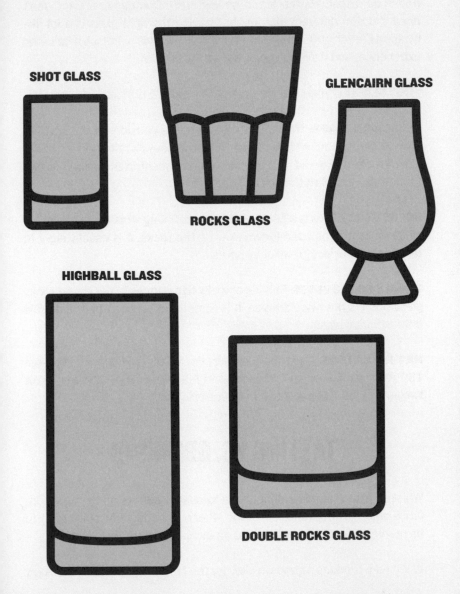

SHOT GLASS

ROCKS GLASS

GLENCAIRN GLASS

HIGHBALL GLASS

DOUBLE ROCKS GLASS

neat, water and ice back. I generally swirl the whiskey first. Then I look at its color and legs, meaning how viscous the whiskey is. Then I nose the whiskey. World-famous master distiller Dave Pickerell once told me never to stick your nose into a glass of whiskey as it's an easy way to blow out your olfactory glands for the rest of the day/night. Rather, pass the glass back and forth beneath your nose. Then put the glass to one side of your nose and smell with one nostril. Then do it with the other side.

Take a small sip of the whiskey. Savor it. What do you taste? Grain? Bread? Fruits? Sweets? When people put names to what they are smelling, they are just trying to remember what those smells remind them of. Caramel smells like caramel. Vanilla smells like vanilla. Sometimes you get notes of citrus, or apples and pears. There are many smells. There are no right or wrong answers.

Take a small sip of water. Swallow some of it but not all of it. Then take another sip. Now you are tasting the whiskey.

Now we discover the value of water. Water is added to whiskey in order to mix with it. This does two things. It enhances the nose. You will smell more fragrances in your whiskey once you take a sip of water. Secondly, it will enhance flavors in the whiskey. But don't add a lot of water. Stick your finger in the glass of water and add a few drops of it to the whiskey. Literally, two or three drops. Then swirl it around.

From there, I like to put in one rock, and swirl it around. Some experts claim that the cold will dumb down some of the aromas and flavors. But screw them; I want to start enjoying my whiskey. I swirl the ice and taste the whiskey again. Maybe I'll leave it like that, or maybe I'll add more rocks. Now we're drinking whiskey.

How to Smoke a Glass

There's a whole world out there of folks who love smoke in their whiskey or in their cocktails. It is a relatively popular new trick to add smoke to different whiskies and drinks. And there are numerous ways to do so. You can smoke only the glass, smoke the entire cocktail, or pour smoke into a glass of whiskey or into a cocktail.

I am no bartender or mixologist. But there are plenty of references about how to do this, either in written or video form on the internet. See which one works for you. Make sure when you're smoking a drink you use only woods approved for food use—maple, cherry, or applewood tend to be the best and are usually available in the grilling section of online retailers. *Do not use lumber! Big mistake!*

ENJOYING WHISKEY

Sometimes you just want to have a glass of whiskey and watch the fire, sports, a movie—or maybe put on some music. This is for when you don't mind being alone with your thoughts. It's about having time for yourself. Maybe it's at dusk. Maybe it's a nightcap. Maybe it's just a well-deserved treat.

But some of the best moments are when you share a bottle of whiskey with a good friend or a special someone. There's nothing like chewing on about old times. Favorite moments. Rehashing funny stories, remembering loved ones. Sharing a success or salving yourself after a tough loss. Old friends are great to share a bottle with. And so is that special person. The one who captures your imagination, your eye, your heart. Sharing a glass of whiskey on the deck, out by the firepit, on the sofa with a blanket, or while watching a sunset. Sharing that intimate moment over a glass of whiskey can be one of life's great pleasures.

And sometimes it's a party. A group of good friends. A barbecue, a cookout, a dinner party, an anniversary, a birthday, the holidays. There are so many events to celebrate and to break out a special bottle or two to share. Let the laughs and the stories roll. It's always a good time to share whiskey.

A lot of people ask me, "What is the best bottle of whiskey?" Or wine? Or beer? My answer is always the same. It's the bottle you like. Inexpensive, medium priced, a hundred dollars a bottle or more, it doesn't matter. It's the one you like that you should opt for. Many of my most memorable bottles have been medium priced, along with a few rare or expensive ones.

But to me it's more about who you share it with. What the occasion is. Whiskey is about sharing with other people. That's the beauty of whiskey.

WHISKEY WITH FOOD

Generally speaking, as with wine, lighter whiskies go with lighter fare. Heavier whiskies go with more robust fare.

Cheese, salami, and bread generally go well with whiskey. Why? Because the fats and salt balance out the mouth, which can take quite a beating during a whiskey tasting session. A few bites in between sips are always a welcomed respite. It resets the palate, and you're ready to taste new whiskies all over again. You really can never go wrong with these.

Peanuts are a popular bar offering. So are Chex Mix and Asian cocktail snack medleys. Again, fats, oils, and salts offer the palate a reset while drinking and provide a great counterbalance to the whiskey.

Sushi, maki, sashimi, and other Asian cuisines pair better with lighter whiskies such as a lighter-styled Japanese whisky, a Scotch blend, single grain, a Highlands single malt, or a nice young rye whiskey. In Japan, especially at business dinners, the guests will have whisky and soda, allowing them to enjoy the evening without over-imbibing.

If you're eating dinner or lunch, fish is a wonderful side with a glass of whiskey. Salmon, bass, and trout all go very well with single malt, Japanese whiskies, and high rye whiskies. Again, the fat and flavors of the fish juxtapose beautifully with the whiskies. On the other hand, canned smoked oysters, fresh or smoked fish, mackerel, salmon, and sardines often prove a good match for Islay single malts, which have bigger flavors.

Of course, whiskey is always a good partner for steak. A filet mignon, New York strip, ribeye, or porterhouse, with their rich accompanying sauces and/or fatty content, are a great match for almost any whiskey. And Highland Scotches and Japanese single malts go beautifully with Kobe or Wagyu beef. Outstanding!

All whiskies are not necessarily created equal when it comes to food pairings. For example, single malt Scotch does not pair as well with BBQ as bourbon and Tennessee whiskey do. And single malt Scotch and Scotch blends definitely match better with haggis or a lovely rack of lamb.

When it comes to dessert, bourbon and Scotch play very nicely with chocolate. In fact, when you go to Kentucky and Tennessee or Scotland, many tasting rooms and/or distillery gift shops will offer chocolate that has been infused with their whiskey.

Single malt also pairs well with such treats as apple pie, shortbread cookies, vanilla ice cream, and mince pie, to name a few. Bourbon goes beautifully with pumpkin pie, sweet potato pie, and pecan pie as well as with shortbread and vanilla ice cream.

FINAL THOUGHTS

My father had one steadfast rule—he felt sugar and sweetness had no real place in the world of alcohol. No matter the medium, he preferred his beverages dry. "Don't give me any of that sweet shit," he would repeatedly say. I only saw him order an Old Fashioned once or twice in my life. He liked a Rob Roy. Or a Manhattan. Maybe a Boulevardier. But nothing sweet. He didn't like bourbon. Dry Scotch was his game. A traditionalist. He would take that first sip of a cocktail or that first sip of whiskey like he was taking communion in church. No matter the place, it was almost reverential. Like it was in slow motion. He would bend toward the bar, bring the glass to his lips, take that first sip, and stop to relish it. He'd close his eyes, and even sometimes whistle. Then he'd pick his head up, and he was ready to chat. The appetizers could wait on the table.

My father was tall, 6'2", and weighed in at about 200 pounds. He was Steve McQueen. He was Dino. Money. Cars. Looks. He loved to party. He could talk sports and politics with the guys. And he was an elegant dancer, much admired by the ladies. I've only begun to realize now that, had we met when we were the same age, he would have been one of the cool guys, and I would have been the bookish geek. He was not a perfect man. But I loved him terribly despite it.

Many years ago now, he was diagnosed with stage 4 liver cancer. He was 76. His prognosis was not good. Two to four months. When I first talked to him, not sure what to say, he shrugged his shoulders. "It's all part of life, kid. We all gotta do it." Privately, I cried. He said on several occasions, "I'm gonna see my dad." He was a better man than I all the way to the end. He rarely showed emotion. Anger, yes. Weakness, rarely. He wanted no wake. To him, there was nothing worse than yet another stiff at a party.

Not long before the end, I was trying to help him shave his weathered face, bristling with gray. He clutched his belly in pain. Looking to defuse the moment, I told him that it reminded me of the movie *The Bucket List*. He angrily asked what the hell I was talking about. There was real anger in his eyes as he grimaced again. I reminded him that in the movie, Nicholson was throwing up on the floor of a bathroom. He was doubled over in pain from chemotherapy. When he finally stood up, he looked in the mirror and said to himself, "Boy, somewhere, some lucky guy is having a heart attack." My father burst out in his classic loud laugh, slapping the bathroom counter and guffawing. It had done the trick. And he hugged me.

We all sat with my father, a day or two before the end, in the hospital, the hospice ward, watching him slowly fade. A big, strong, handsome man laid low by time and disease. An endless parade of family and friends all came to bid him farewell. He slept through most of it. He would wake up, saying the dog needed to be let out, or telling us to answer the door. Nonsense.

Afterward, when he was given morphine, he fell asleep comfortably for the first time in days. It was then the rest of us decided to go out to dinner. Of course, we went to the bar first. We all needed a drink, and ordered cocktails. I couldn't drink Rob Roys or Manhattans back then (they are the only thing I'll drink now . . . the acorn and the tree). I had an Old Fashioned (he didn't like those—too sweet) but I toasted him nonetheless. And we sat at the bar and talked. The appetizers could wait.

MOONSHINE

My first memory of moonshine includes my old neighbor and friend, Ralph Cooley. Ralph grew up in the country, and I got to know him because I had bought his family's old farm. Ralph's family hadn't lived there for a generation, but we were looking to restore it to a working farm, and Ralph was happy to help out. He was invaluable.

One Saturday night, exhausted from a day of working on the farm, I was in bed and asleep at 10 p.m. when I got a phone call. It was Ralph inviting me to a bonfire.

"You're having a bonfire now?" I asked, my wife and I buried under the covers.

"Hell, yeah! Get your ass up! Come on down!" he bellowed.

I demurred several times. "Where is this bonfire?" I finally asked.

"In your backyard!" he laughed and hung up. *What the hell?* I quickly got dressed and ran downstairs and outside. There, around the firepit, were Ralph and a few friends, with a massive fire raging. And there were two jugs. He passed me a one-gallon plastic milk jug filled with some kind of brown juice.

"What the hell is this?" I asked, exasperated.

"Apple pie moonshine. Homemade!" he announced proudly. I rolled my eyes. I was a wine guy at the time. I had no interest in hooch. But I didn't want to be rude, so I took a sip. Oh my god! It was as low-down a drink as I could think up. Fresh apple cider, cinnamon, and moonshine. But I loved it. Fine-quality booze? Maybe not. But fun around a campfire? You betcha!

We stayed up until all hours, swapping stories about the farm and the new challenges, talking of trucks and dogs and tractors. And all the while, chugging away at the sweet brown juice in that big plastic jug. And later, from a mason jar, I got a taste of the straight stuff. Smooth. Clean. Crisp. I don't remember more than the first few hours of that night, sitting in the backyard, watching the flames climb toward a sky filled with stars and hearing the stories and laughter.

I woke up early the next morning, around 5 a.m., with the gray light coming up and the fire smoldering. I had two blankets over me, still in the Adirondack chair I had settled into the night before. Ralph and his friends had gone home and just left me there. That was my initiation into moonshine. It was fun as hell.

MOONSHINE 101

White whiskey. Moonshine. Corn whiskey. White lightning. Corn liquor. What's the difference? Moonshine is the generic term that was originally ascribed to illegal hooch. The name dates all the way back to folks in Scotland who did not want to pay the king's taxes on distilled spirits, so they would make it at night in the woods, by moonlight. This distilling tradition was transported to America through the great migrations of Scottish and Irish immigrants to the New World.

On this side of the pond, moonshine has come to be known by a lot of other colorful names, including bootleg, firewater, branch water, white lightning, kickapoo, shine, Happy Sally, ruckus juice, joy juice, hooch, panther's breath, mountain dew, hillbilly pop, pop skull, skull cracker, bush wisky, stump, mule kick, catdaddy, cool water, old horsey, rotgut, wildcat, rise 'n' shine, splo, and many more.

Moonshine is romantic. It's dangerous. It's exciting. It's down home. It's got stories—lots of stories. Perhaps no other distilled product has as many as moonshine.

Moonshine has featured greatly in American history, including the Whiskey Rebellion in Pennsylvania in 1794 (provoked when the U.S. government enacted a liquor tax), several well-known hill feuds, Prohibition, and the birth of NASCAR. Moonshine's connection to NASCAR extends all the way back to the 1940s and 1950s, when moonshiners revved up their cars to outrace lawmen. Eventually, they began racing against each other to see who was the fastest, and a sport was born—all from carrying cases of moonshine.

The making of moonshine has also attracted some memorable characters, like 400-pound Mahala Mullins (who once offered cookies and milk to revenuers sent to arrest her), Dutch Schultz, Junior Johnson, and Popcorn Sutton. And it even spawned popular television shows like *Moonshiners*.

"You can tell a lot about a man by the shine he makes."

—Legendary moonshiner Popcorn Sutton

Today, moonshine is used to describe a segment of the whiskey market, the result of the Alcohol and Tobacco Tax and Trade Bureau (TTB) allowing commercially made unaged whiskey to be called moonshine. The problem is that not all "moonshines" are alike and this has created confusion in the market. There are four categories of unaged whiskies, or moonshines:

SHINE OR SUGAR WASH: This is made with 100 percent refined sugar, and became prevalent during the 1920s. The sugar results in a certain degree of smoothness. It is a super simple whiskey, easy to drink, little to no nose.

CORN AND CANE: A mash bill of corn and some refined sugar. (Technically, if there is more sugar than corn, it should be called Cane & Corn.) This presents hints of butter and cereal.

CORN WHISKEY: Also known as corn liquor or white dog, corn whiskey is the cornerstone of Kentucky and Tennessee distilling, the bedrock of the industry. It is made from a mash bill that is at least 51 percent corn (usually much higher), and is blended with other grains, most frequently barley and rye. These three components make up the mash bill of 85 to 90 percent of the bourbons and sour mashes made in the region. Some whiskies we know include wheat, but they are rare in the white whiskey category, and are usually turned into bourbon. White whiskey (also known as corn whiskey) is distilled around 160 proof (80 percent ABV). The good corn whiskies have a nose of buttered popcorn and cream of wheat or cornflakes.

UNAGED RYE, UNAGED WHEAT WHISKEY, AND BOURBON MASH: These are new entrants to the category, though they usually end up in the whiskey, not the moonshine, section. Unaged rye has a mash bill of at least 51 percent rye. Bourbon mash usually figures at least 51 percent corn, plus rye and malted barley.

In the beginning, moonshine was a quick way for start-up distillers to generate cash while their whiskies aged. But these days, there are some very good moonshines and white whiskies being made. Indeed, for aficionados of this spirit, eastern Kentucky and eastern Tennessee have become the Napa and Sonoma of moonshine.

What follows are some of my favorite picks from each of the categories.

NOTABLE EXPRESSION — SUGAR WASH

Dutch's Spirits Sugar Wash Moonshine

Perhaps no gangster was more closely associated with Prohibition and illegal beer and hooch in New York City than Arthur Simon Flegenheimer, otherwise known as "Dutch Schultz." Through turf wars and attrition, Dutch became the undisputed king of illegal alcohol in New York City.

Since his death in 1935, rumors have proliferated about the whereabouts of his buried treasure up near the craggy ranges of the Catskill Mountains. In 2010, Schultz's underground distillery was unearthed and outfitted for public view in Pine Plains, New York, at the 400-acre Harvest Homestead Farm. A new distillery was also erected. Dutch's Spirits Sugar Wash Moonshine is a nod to the bottled lightning made in that cavernous distillery. It is made from turbinado cane sugar in small artisanal copper pot stills. The moonshine is clean and smooth, with notes of cotton candy, maple, and vanilla. It's not sweet at all and has a nice long finish. A super versatile spirit. Great for shots. Great on the rocks. And great in cocktails. A superior example of 100 percent sugar moonshine.

NOTABLE EXPRESSIONS — CORN & CANE

Ole Smoky Blue Flame Tennessee Moonshine

Ole Smoky became the first federally licensed distillery in the history of East Tennessee, and was only the fourth distillery licensed in the state when it opened on July 4, 2010. It quickly became the poster child for craft distilling, and proved the market for moonshine was ripe for the picking—it is the most visited distillery in the world, with more than five million visitors coming through their four locations each year. That's more than Jack Daniel's, or the entirety of the distilleries on the Kentucky Bourbon Trail.

Ole Smoky's current recipe has been tweaked and rejiggered with the help of master distiller Dave Pickerell, who was previously the master distiller at Maker's Mark (and went on to oversee such successful whiskies as Hillrock Estate and WhistlePig, among others). The ingredients are locally sourced. This moonshine starts with a corn mash left over from corn whiskey production. The distillery adds sugar and water back to the corn and lets it re-ferment. The product takes its name from the old moonshiner's habit of lighting up their product to prove its purity; supposedly, a blue flame was proof of it (it wasn't).

Take a sip. The yeast comes across first, like cornbread. There are hints of sugar and spice in the nose as well. This is a strong, clear spirit, but has notes of sweet cereal, bread, and some lovely floral notes. The taste of this ends with a hot punch to the mouth and a smooth, clean finish. It's also extremely versatile, great on the rocks and in cocktails.

Sugarlands Shine Silver Cloud Tennessee Sour Mash Moonshine

Sugarlands Distilling Co. is the second best-selling brand of moonshine in the U.S. Made with Tennessee corn and cane sugar, Silver Cloud is a tremendous moonshine. At 100 proof, it's subtle and smooth. Hints of corn and butter, with a lovely, creamy softness, this moonshine is easy to drink on the rocks with a twist or paired with a fun mixer. Amazing stuff.

Twin Creeks Distillery 1st Sugar Moonshine

Located in the hills of Franklin County, Virginia, Twin Creeks Distillery keeps the tradition alive. Except, instead of corn, these folks run a sugar wash over leftover rye from making rye whiskey. Strong, smooth, and spicy, there are hints of apple, caramel, and lots of hot spice on the finish. This is great for making cocktails or sipping on the rocks. A stellar hooch just shy of whiskey.

Dumplin Creek 140.7 Moonshine

Dumplin Creek is a classic corn & cane moonshine made by Old Tennessee Distilling Co. This shine is named for Exit 407 on I-40 (also for its proof, 140.7), which leads to one of the most popular tourist destinations in eastern Tennessee, Sevierville, nestled near Great Smoky Mountains National Park, and home to Old Tennessee. The whiskey is super, super smooth, with light notes of butter and corn, and finishes clean. Great as a mixer or on lots of ice.

NOTABLE EXPRESSION — CORN WHISKEY

Midnight Moon 100 Proof Moonshine

The link between NASCAR and moonshine is legendary. One of the biggest of those legends was Junior Johnson. Johnson hailed from a family of moonshiners. His was a generation determined to deliver their product to thirsty customers and hell-bent on outracing the law enforcement trying to keep them from doing that. Junior Johnson was never caught while transporting the goods. He and other speedsters brought their skills to the racetrack in the 1950s, and Johnson became one of the legends of NASCAR. Midnight Moon 100 Proof is inspired by Johnson's family moonshine recipe. This spirit is made from American corn, and it offers an ultrasmooth palate, with notes of corn and vanilla and a hint of spice at the back. Crisp and clean. A great sipper that can stand up to rocks.

Buffalo Trace Distillery White Dog

Buffalo Trace's White Dog is new-make bourbon that hasn't been aged. It's clear and usually has a mash bill of more than 51 percent corn, with a mixture of rye and a small amount of malted barley. Of all the white whiskies listed here, it has the most complex flavor. Notes of corn and vanilla dominate, but hints of apple and pear may come across. The mouthfeel and flavor are more pronounced. There is pepper and other spices at the back end but a creamy smoothness lingers.

A FEW MORE TO CONSIDER

Other good corn whiskies to try are George Dickel White Corn Whisky Foundation Recipe, Hartfield & Co. White Whiskey, and Nelson's Green Brier Tennessee Handmade White Whiskey

UNAGED RYE AND WHEAT WHITE WHISKIES

Old Natchez Trace White Tennessee Whiskey

Old Natchez Trace is made by Lee Kennedy, at Leiper's Fork Distillery in Tennessee. His white whiskey is one of the most complex I have ever had, made from 100 percent locally sourced grain—70 percent rye, 22 percent corn, and 8 percent malted barley. Big notes of white pepper and spice, hints of anise and a gingersnap ending. Drink neat or with one ice cube. This one is only available at the distillery—a good reason to visit!

Dad's Hat Pennsylvania White Rye

Bottled at 100 proof, this one is a big, bold slap in the face. Made in Pennsylvania, it's 80 percent rye, 5 percent malted rye, and 15 percent malted barley. Spicy and complex, it makes a great Bloody Mary, but is also special just on the rocks with a twist or your favorite vodka mixer.

Drift Unaged Wheat Whiskey

One of the more unique offerings of unaged wheat whiskey. The distillery is in San Clemente, California, but the hard red Winter Wheat used to make it is grown on the owner's parents' farm in Kansas. This award-winning white whiskey is super smooth, with notes of vanilla and cereal. Great alone, on the rocks, or perfect in a Highball with ginger ale and a twist of your favorite citrus.

Barrel-Aged Moonshine

Most whiskey purists turn their nose up at the thought of such a suggestion. Moonshine aged in bourbon barrels, especially used bourbon barrels, is a monstrosity to them, not worth reviewing. But many craft distilleries put aside some of their unaged whiskey to sell as moonshine in order to pay their bills and keep the lights on until their bourbon matures. Several small distillers have been brave enough to age their moonshines in bourbon barrels.

This idea of aging moonshine has for a very long time been part of the home vatting market, with aficionados buying barrel aging kits (available at home brewing stores, catalogs, and online). One can either buy charred oak chips or sticks to put in a bottle or buy a small oak barrel (from 1 liter to 1.25 gallons) in which to age the hooch. Of course, the idea goes back much further than that. Many a great-great-grandfather who made shine barrel aged some of it at one point or another. This is just one more trick out of the old rucksack.

The barrel-aged bottles that have been super popular include Boundary Oak Distillery's Patton Armored Diesel and Casey Jones Moonshine Barrel Cut. These elixirs are super easy to drink and infinitely smooth. They are like light whiskies, though they can still pack a wallop where alcohol is concerned, but often without the burn—called the Kentucky Hug—that one usually associates with bourbon or rye.

HOW TO DRINK MOONSHINE

Unaged spirits are often guffawed at, which is completely asinine. Quality corn whiskies can be very sophisticated, elegant, complex sippers, like a good vodka, though they are slightly oilier and chewier than vodka, as are unaged rye and bourbon mash.

Put the mason jars away and pull out your rocks glasses. Enjoy moonshine over ice. Sugar wash and corn & cane are perfect for making homemade apple pie moonshine; just combine them with cider and a hint of cinnamon. Moonshine is also tasty mixed with fruit punch—or almost anything fruity and sweet. You can substitute moonshine for vodka in most any cocktail that involves mixers. It makes a great whiskey sour (it's also fantastic in a margarita or dirty martini) and is terrific with tonic.

BOURBON

came from a background of blended Scotch; my introduction to bourbon came much later. It was in the late aughts when my interest in American whiskey began to take hold. I went on a bourbon kick. I tried a lot of them.

I'd been hanging out with Clay Risen, *New York Times* reporter and editor and author of multiple books on whiskey, trying hooch from all around the country in extensive tasting sessions. Each taster would get a printed sheet with numerous boxes to fill out and at least fifty descriptors down at the bottom, plus plenty of room to write down our impressions on color, smell, taste, and finish. There were also questions and prompts to respond to. It was a very educational and enlightening experience, approaching whiskey the way many professional wine writers rate wines. I also learned pretty quickly, I was a lightweight.

I pride myself on drinking local, so when I started to get my local bourbon jones goin', I decided to try the bourbons of the Hudson Valley and New England, closer to where I lived. I visited Hillrock Estate, Catskill Mountain Distillery, Tuthilltown Spirits, and, eventually, Finger Lakes Distilling and Taconic Distillery, and the like.

One of my most memorable visits from this early period was with Rich Srsich to Berkshire Mountain Distillers, in Massachusetts. The distillery had just launched its Cask Finished series. Distiller and owner Chris Weld had collaborated with ten influential craft brewers that included Samuel Adams, Founders Brewing Co., Ommegang, and Hale's Ales to finish bourbons in former beer barrels. Each finish resulted in a hugely different whiskey. Tasting them was an eye-opening experience. I remember driving home from that tasting. We were so shaky that we stopped at a roadside farm-to-table hotdog stand half-a-mile down the road, and each ate two large dogs with sodas and milkshakes. We stayed there for a while until we got ourselves right. It was a great day with an old friend.

Bourbon remains America's most well-known and popularly consumed barrel-aged distilled spirit. As of 2020, bourbon accounted for half of all the whiskey sales in the United States. And no region is more closely associated with this American classic than Kentucky. It is the epicenter of whiskey in the United States; it is the Napa, the Scotland, the Bordeaux of American whiskey. It is, simply, "The Bourbon Capital of the World."

America and Kentucky are currently in their second golden age of bourbon. The rise of its popularity and the demand for new product has been meteoric since the turn of this last century. In 2009 there were nineteen distilleries in production. In August 2016 there were over 52 producing whiskey, with more in the planning and licensing stages. Many are small craft distilleries, but a good number are planned as large volume production facilities.

BOURBON 101

When it comes to bourbon, there are four main grains we are concerned with: corn, malted barley, rye, and wheat. These grains, in some combination, are the backbone of the industry. Corn is central to Kentucky bourbon. Dent corn is the coin of the realm, and the cornfields of the South and Midwest feed a steady stream of it to distilleries throughout these two regions. But in recent years, many smaller boutique distilleries (and even some larger ones) have begun to branch out, reaching back to heritage corn varieties to provide distinctive flavors to distinguish their whiskies. Most of these are dent corn—also known as grain corn—a type of field corn with a high soft-starch content. It is so named because of the small indentation ("dent") that develops at the crown of each kernel. Some of the more obscure heirloom varieties now being planted for use in whiskey, especially bourbon, include Bloody Butcher, Blue Corn, Tennessee Red Cob, Wapsie Valley, Missouri Meerschaum

Pipe, Pencil Cob, Jimmy Red, Boone County White, and Neon Pink popcorn. See the profile on page 54 of Balcones Distilling's blue corn—based whiskies.

Rye finds its way into 90 percent of the bourbon produced in this country. It offers the spicy notes that one associates with a gingersnap-like quality or a peppery finish.

Malted barley is almost always in the bourbon mix, providing several different elements. First, it adds softer nutty, smoky, and sometimes chocolatey notes. And because the barley is malted (which means it has been wetted and begun to germinate), it supplies enzymes that will help break down the grains and aid the yeast in turning the sugars and carbohydrates into alcohol. Some people think bourbon must be made in Kentucky, or it cannot be called bourbon. Not true. According to federal regulations, bourbon can be made anywhere in the United States. Federal standards state that bourbon made for U.S. consumption must be:

- **Produced in the U.S. or its territories, as well as the District of Columbia**
- **Made from a grain mixture that is at least 51 percent corn**
- **Aged in charred new oak containers**
- **Distilled to no more than 160 (U.S.) proof (80% ABV)**
- **Entered into the container for aging at no more than 125 proof (62.5% ABV)**
- **Bottled (like other whiskies) at 80 proof or more (40% ABV)**

HOW TO DRINK BOURBON— ACCORDING TO BOURBON ROYALTY

If you are lucky, when you go visit Buffalo Trace's immense operation you will be given the tour by bourbon industry legend Freddie Johnson, a third-generation employee at the distillery—his grandfather, James B. "Jimmy" Johnson Sr., was the first African American foreman in Kentucky and worked at the distillery until 1964.

Now, I must admit, when I began editing and writing about spirits long ago, I had no idea who Freddie Johnson was. And when I decided to visit Buffalo Trace for the first time, I still didn't know—I had set up an appointment with Harlen Wheatley, the master distiller. When we got to the distillery, a young lady came out, and said there had been a change of plans and we would be given the tour by Freddie. I think she might have assumed that if I was writing about bourbon, I already knew. But I had no clue, and felt kind of miffed: Why was the master distiller blowing me off on some tour guide?

As I began to follow Freddie around, it was clear he knew everything about the place. And everywhere we went with him, people would wave, come over and say hello, give him a hug, or pull him aside for some special, quiet conversation. Freddie always ended these tête-à-têtes with a smile and a handshake.

At one point we ended up on the barreling line. Buffalo Trace rolls out barrels at the same rate Apple makes iPhones. It is an industrial operation as much as it is a quality producer. As the barrels are rolled down the line, they are checked for leaks. If one is leaking, a cooper will plug the hole right there, tapping in small bits of toothpick until the bleeding stops. And then they are pushed on down the line.

It is impressive in its efficiency, a fact that threatens to overshadow the artistry at play. And if Freddie had not taught me more than a thing or two on that tour, I might have missed all that Buffalo Trace's bourbon has to offer. It is a no-age-statement spirit but is generally believed to be a blend of whiskies between eight and ten years old. The taste is smooth and flavorful, with brown sugar, vanilla, and toffee. A touch of oak and spice. This is a great sipping whiskey, straight or over ice. Simple, easy, and always good for a glass or two. A great bourbon to tell stories over.

To Freddie, bourbon is not just a tag on a bottle of whiskey. He once told whiskey journalist Melissa Alexander, "For every day that we walk this earth, there will always be more barrels of bourbon being made. But friends and family will not always be nearby. So when you bring the bottle out, enjoy the moment, because that's what bourbon is made for." Freddie explained that there are several secrets to tasting bourbon, especially when sampling high-proof, cask-strength bourbon.

"Firstly, make sure you jostle a bottle of cask-strength bourbon before you pour it. There may be some sediment in the bottle. You want your guests to have some of that sediment. It is part of the whiskey, and should be something they experience. It is slight, and hard to see, but it is often there. Especially expensive bourbons, which tend to sit for a long time on people's bars without being touched. Just a gentle turn of the bottle, maybe tilting it sideways gently.

"First, take a very, very small sip of the whiskey. Let it sit on your tongue. Swish it around a touch. Now swallow. When you swallow the whiskey,

DO NOT INHALE! Calmly exhale. Let all that alcohol out before you breathe in. This not only reduces the burn of whiskey, especially high-proof whiskey, but allows more air to get at the whiskey so you can taste it better.

"Now, take a small sip of water. Very small. Hold just the slightest bit of water on your tongue for a second. Just a good enough coating on your tongue to know it's still wet. Then take another small sip of whiskey. Let that blend with the water on your tongue and swish it around. Swallow and exhale again.

"Now, you will truly taste the whiskey."

This is how Freddie Johnson tastes bourbon. And when I am down in Kentucky, I always go to visit him. As Freddie always says, "Keep making memories!"

"Whisky is liquid sunshine"

—George Bernard Shaw

NOTABLE EXPRESSIONS

W. L. Weller Antique 107

Also from Buffalo Trace is my favorite wheated bourbon, Weller. I love wheated bourbons (which use wheat instead of rye in the mash) but not in cocktails, as I feel it's the rye that helps bourbon stand out in any given drink recipe. Wheated bourbons tend to fade into the background. On the other hand, I think wheated bourbons are the absolute best sippers, real easy drinking. Neat, with a hint of water, or even a rock or two of ice (don't overdo it).

Weller Antique 107 is estimated to be 70 percent corn, 16 percent wheat, and 14 percent malted barley. Wheat replaces the edge that rye usually supplies with soft notes of vanilla. Weller is aged far longer than most wheated bourbons in the market. This particular expression is aged approximately six to seven years. The 107 is representative of the proof of the bottling.

Super smooth, well balanced, and a lovely deep bronze color, Weller Antique 107 has aromas of lanolin, almond, creamed corn, and toasty vanilla. The midpalate flavor is heavily wheated, layered, and moderately sweet. The finish is long, oaky, and intensely smooth. It's a great bottle to pour for special friends.

Some other favorite wheated bourbons include the bestseller in the category, Maker's Mark, as well as Larceny and Old Fitzgerald.

Russell's Reserve

I will never forget when I was traveling through Kentucky and posted on my social media that I was at Wild Turkey, one of the most iconic whiskey brands in the world, producing such labels as Rare Bird, Master's Keep, and Kentucky Spirit. This was maybe the second year Russell's Reserve was out. The messages on my cellphone suddenly blew up. Every spirit geek I knew wanted some specific bottle of Russell's Reserve, bourbon or rye.

Russell's Reserve was rolled out in 2013, co-created by Jimmy and Eddie Russell. Two more famous distillers there are not. Between them they had ninety-plus years of experience. This father/son team of master distillers brought Wild Turkey to new levels of achievement during their tenure.

The idea behind Russell's Reserve was to produce a non–chill filtered bourbon and rye to compete in the high-end spirits portion of the market. Russell's Reserve is an expression of Jimmy and Eddie's favorite bourbon and rye whiskies. These whiskies are made using the traditional house mash bills. "Every expression of Russell's Reserve—both the bourbon and rye whiskey—is matured in only the deepest no. 4 or 'alligator' charred American white oak barrels," according to the Russells, ensuring richness of flavor and color.

Russell's Reserve Single Barrel Kentucky Straight Bourbon Whiskey (110 proof/55% ABV) is loaded with flavor. It has a smooth start and a lip-smacking end and is aged eight to ten years. Russell's Reserve 10 Year Old Kentucky Bourbon Whiskey (90 proof/45% ABV) is aged in Char-4 barrels, and bottled at 90 proof. Both are big, rich, smooth, creamy, spicy, complex, and incredibly drinkable whiskies; the 10 Year Old is something special, as it has retained a little more of the classic bourbon sweetness. Lots of dates, nuts, figs, vanilla, and toffee. The single barrel is amazingly smooth, with a lovely finish that gives you that great "Kentucky hug" without the burn. Do not hesitate to purchase them if given the opportunity.

Kentucky Peerless Distilling Co.

In the 1880s, Peerless was a powerful brand and a regional powerhouse. In 1917, it was knocking out 200 barrels of whiskey a day and approximately 23,000 barrels annually. The label was laid low by Prohibition. In 2009, Corky Taylor insisted on reestablishing this forgotten brand that his great-grandfather owned from 1896 to 1917.

Peerless is made using sweet mash, instead of sour mash, the industry standard. In sour mash, you take some of yesterday's yeast and put it together with today's yeast to ensure quality and consistency. In sweet mash, you pitch new yeast every day. At Peerless, there's no cold filtration, and everything is bottled at barrel proof.

Why sweet mash? "Starting with fresh ingredients every single time, as we do with a sweet mash, eliminates any crossover between the two. So there's intrinsically a cleaner break doing a sweet mash than there would be if we were doing a sour mash," said master distiller and bourbon prodigy Caleb Kilburn. "That makes us a little more nimble as far as being able to switch between products and remain consistent because the first cook of a sweet mash should be, in theory, nearly identical to the hundredth."

They also place their spirits in the barrel at 107 proof, much lower than many other producers. Caleb's goal is that the flavor be as robust as possible since all their bottlings are sold at cask strength. He argues that there is no dilution of the flavor at bottling.

Peerless is a unique tasting experience, with a flavor profile that features sweet tobacco, apples and pears, candied apricots, citrus zest, butterscotch, French vanilla, caramel, white pepper, and a hint of Christmas spice. You definitely want to try these whiskies. While Peerless is a big whiskey, and begs to be tried neat or on a single rock, you can absolutely make terrific cocktails with it. I prefer rye in my Old Fashioned, but this whiskey can stand out in that glass too!

Angel's Envy and the Evolution of Bourbon

As the market for bourbon grew from 2000 to 2020 and beyond, distillers realized that they needed to up their game. Making bourbon with the requisite 51 percent (or more) corn, rye, and malted barley produced a classic American spirit but, as store shelves filled and competition grew stiffer, there was a need to differentiate. Single barrel, cask strength releases made their appearance, then finished bourbons. And distillers have pushed even further. Here are a few makers who stand out for their contributions to the industry.

Set in the middle of downtown Louisville, opposite Louisville Slugger Field, nestled among the office buildings of this fine old city, Angel's Envy is certainly the envy of anyone who wants to be in the distilling business.

Its incredibly well-appointed gift shop and education center are the height of sleek and modern industrial glam. The upstairs event space is otherworldly, a combination of Beaux-Arts and the National Parks Service, with massive windows cased in steel, copper, and brick overlooking the city and the Ohio River. It is nothing short of breathtaking.

But despite the dazzling views and architecture, Angel's Envy is all about genes. It is hard to start a distillery with a better pedigree than this one has. The late Lincoln Henderson, and his son, Wes Henderson, both spent many years building various whiskey brands.

Lincoln Henderson was one of the most storied master distillers in the history of the region. He created such premium products as Gentleman Jack and Jack Daniel's Single Barrel, as well as Woodford Reserve (with Chris Morris at his side). He guided much of the distilling program at Brown-Forman for nearly forty years.

Lincoln retired in the mid-1990s. When the new craft distilling boom began to take off in the early 2000s, Wes went to visit his father with a crazy idea—they should start a distillery of their own. Lincoln had never had that kind of backing or control. And so their experiments with mash and finishing began, with Lincoln combing through his legendary black book for ideas.

"Wes, you started this thing, I'm here to help you, I'll help any way I can. You let me know where and when you need me," Lincoln told his son.

"And that's what I do with my sons," Wes said later. "You jump right in and get your feet wet. You enjoy your successes, make your mistakes, learn from those mistakes and then just keep going forward."

When the first experimental barrels were ready to taste, Lincoln opened them only to find that the angels had taken a heavy share through evaporation. Once they tasted the whiskey inside, Lincoln declared that the angels should envy him and Wes. The whiskey that had been left behind was superb. And that's the origin of the distillery's name.

In the beginning the whiskey was made to Lincoln's specific instructions and formula. The small production run was an immediate hit. While it makes bourbon the old-fashioned way, Angel's Envy is a port-finished product, meaning that the bourbon, which first rests in charred American white oak, then spends additional time in port casks, acquiring a softer, rounder finish that gives it a brandy or cognac feel.

With the American bourbon market bursting at the seams, growth lay elsewhere. How to dominate a foreign market first? Bourbon needed to be able to compete with single malt Scotch, cognac, and numerous other brown spirits, but lacked the cachet. Champagne, cognac, and single malt in a duty-free shop were winners. Bourbon? Not so much. Thus, the industry needed to up its game. Enter Lincoln and Wes. Packaged in a fabulous new bottle (it almost looks more like perfume than bourbon), tagged with a higher price point, and sporting its unique port cask aging, this new whiskey, Angel's Envy, was the answer the bourbon industry had been waiting for.

This was not just a simple marketing ploy. This was genius at work. More than anything, Angel's Envy showed the bourbon world, and the rest of the distilling industry, what a high expression of bourbon could be. Momentum gathered and demand grew. Today Angel's Envy is among the most expensive bourbons in the world. It has succeeded and deservedly so.

The whiskey combines the best of bourbon—notes of corn, oak, caramel, brown sugar—with hints of date, fig, and stone fruit supplied by the port cask. It is an exquisite dram, a sophisticated bourbon.

Sadly, Lincoln has passed on. Of all his many achievements, Angel's Envy is said by many to be his greatest. But I don't think it is; I think it is his family. The family still runs the distillery, which is now owned by liquor giant Bacardi.

"You hear stories all the time about family businesses that have struggles, and that's a natural thing. But some of that conflict is healthy conflict," said Wes. "I love tension. I think tension is a better word for it. I think there's a healthy tension there. And we have that, but we support each other all the way down the line." This spirit is a toast to a great master distiller and his family legacy. A damned fine (and beautiful) bottle of classy whiskey.

Woodford Reserve Double Oaked

Woodford Reserve has a bourbon hall of fame pedigree. The original master distiller was the legendary Lincoln Henderson, and then, for the longest time, Chris Morris. Today Morris and Elizabeth McCall lead this venerable house. Woodford was the first boutique bourbon distillery in Kentucky, modeled in the spirit of The Balvenie in Scotland. Brown-Forman created the distillery to produce a high-end bourbon worthy of an international reputation. The old stone buildings are outfitted with giant copper pot stills, an old Scottish brass-and-glass spirits safe from the 1800s, and huge, outsized leather-bound ledgers that record the daily distilling. It is truly a magical place surrounded by beautifully manicured gardens and lawns. I always say, Woodford is Augusta National without the golf course, and with better whiskey.

I remember my first bottle of Woodford Reserve, which I bought while attending the 2002 Kentucky Derby. I was covering the race and promoting my book about legendary horse trainer D. Wayne Lukas. It had been miserable at Churchill Downs that week, marred by torrential rains, but I made the most of it— I drank mint juleps at least once a day, and discovered the equally popular infield alternative, the super-easy-to-drink bourbon and Ale-8. Woodford was the official bourbon of the race, and everywhere I went I was drinking Woodford Reserve. I became so enamored of it that I bought one of the collectible race bottles to bring home with me. I held on to that bottle for at least eight years, before I opened it up for a group of spirits writers I had visiting.

Since then, I've been lucky enough to visit Woodford and meet with the people who make it. One of the best things about these visits is tasting the fun, new experimental whiskies they are always coming up with. One of my favorites is the Woodford Double Oaked. Originally a tasting room item, and now available regularly, it takes a classic Woodford Reserve bourbon out of the barrel after two years and places it in a heavily toasted new oak barrel for at least another two years.

"Double the maturation, double the wood exposure," said Chris Morris at the time the first bottles were released. In January of 2023, a new limited edition of the whiskey, Double Double Oaked, was released, described as "one of our most-coveted annual bourbon releases." It offers up creamy vanilla, caramel, honey apple, and some lovely Christmas spices. Definitely a holiday bottle to impress friends and family. I love this whiskey.

Hillrock Solera Bourbon

Not all great bourbon is made in Kentucky. One of my absolute favorites is produced in the Hudson Valley, in New York State. I met Jeffrey Baker at Governor Cuomo's Wine, Beer, and Spirits Summit in Albany in 2012. Hillrock is his family farm in Ancram, New York. Jeff was an early advocate of the farm-to-table movement. Hillrock Estate Distillery is one of the few farm-to-glass distilleries in the world. And it is one of a handful in the world to floor malt its own or locally grown grain to produce fine handcrafted spirits on the estate. A financial industry professional, Baker and his wife, Cathy, run this gorgeous estate.

Hillrock is an absolutely unique place, a jewel box of a distillery, set among the rolling hills that ride the eastern edge of the Hudson River. Jeff has hired an incredible team to help run it. With their skills, Hillrock has created immense buzz in the industry. It's a testament to his group. Most notable was his master distiller, the late Dave Pickerell, who was previously the master distiller for Maker's Mark. Dave had more than twenty-five years of experience and was respected worldwide as one of the top master distillers and spirits experts in the industry. Dave provided Hillrock with unmatched industry experience in the areas of product development, business planning, system design, production, staffing/training, operations management, and sales.

There are two things that speak volumes about Hillrock. Firstly, they are totally vertical. They grow the grain, malt their barley, and make their whiskey from what they grow. Second, they use the solera method to make their bourbon, the same method used to create exceptional sherries, ports, Madeiras, and cognacs. Hillrock is the only solera bourbon in the world.

The solera aging technique is centuries old and involves a pyramid of barrels, with a small portion of whiskey removed periodically from the lowest tier of barrels and an equal measure of new whiskey added to the top barrels. No barrel is ever emptied, and over time, the older whiskey mingles with younger whiskies to create unmatched depth and complexity. Twenty-year-old oloroso sherry casks are used. This painstakingly slow process makes this incredible whiskey.

The result is a complex bourbon made for a sophisticated palate. It can compete with any single malt. There are notes of caramel, rye spice, hints of toasted oak, vanilla, but also stone fruit, date, fig, and raisin that linger long after the whiskey has been swallowed. For those single malt drinkers looking for a bourbon that comes close to single malt, this is that complex and well-balanced bourbon.

Balcones Texas Blue Corn Bourbon

Balcones Distilling in Waco, Texas, has been, since its founding in 2008, among the most distinguished, decorated, and acclaimed craft distilleries in America. This cutting-edge house was originally helmed by the iconic Chip Tate, a fanatical, obsessed tinkerer who created some legendary bottles; his Texas Single Malt Whisky was named best in the world in 2013 by the British Best in Glass competition; his classic Rumble Cask Reserve, made with Texas wildflower honey and aged in oak, has won more than a dozen awards; and he is also known for the famed Texas Blue Corn Bourbon.

When talking about this latter invention, Chip said, "I was thinking about bourbon, which is something I love. It's a little bit like barbecue—the meat is certainly important, but when you think about the dominant flavors in barbecue it's really more about smoke and the spice with the rub or the sauce, and bourbon is like that. It just made me wonder out loud, 'What if you made a corn whisky that was supposed to taste like corn? Not moonshine, not bourbon, but something that was aged, refined, and made to almost completely taste like corn?'

"The entire concept of the blue corn whisky was about creating something that, conceptually, sat on the opposite end of the spectrum to the conventional styles of bourbon for which the U.S. is so well known," he explained. "We wanted to focus on a corn whisky whose character and raison d'etre are all about the corn. In keeping with that concept, we sought out the most interesting and flavorful corn we could find, which turned out to be the roasted Hopi blue corn that we now use." Chip pointed to blue corn's rich oiliness and flavor. It is super difficult to work with, but the depth of flavor and distinctiveness seemed worth the effort to Tate.

That's the spirit behind Balcones Texas Blue Corn Bourbon. The whisky is made from 100 percent Texas-grown blue corn. This small-batch, pot-distilled whisky is a big full-bodied mouthful, with a rich mouthfeel and long finish. The color is dark brown, verging on dark cherry. Caramel, toffee, and vanilla lead off the attack. Then the chewiness arrives— dark caramel and molasses, a hint of some indefinable spice, and a dark tea finish. A slow, sweet burn follows. Exquisite.

Chip has since left Balcones, long ago absorbed by a larger entity (it still makes wonderful whiskies), and now heads Tate & Co., also located in Texas. But this whisky continues to carry his mark—big, bold, iconic— like no bourbon you've ever had before. Super impressive. Leave a bottle out when friends come over, especially if a smoker or grill is involved, and see what happens.

TENNESSEE WHISKEY

The best-selling whiskey in the world is a Tennessee whiskey. Ponder that. Two of the oldest surviving labels in American whiskey history are Tennessee whiskies. And all Tennesseans know the truth—the fact that a Tennessee whiskey is the best-selling whiskey in the world sticks in the craw of any Kentucky bourbon colonel. And it ruffles the kilts of more than a few Scots, as well.

Today, Tennessee whiskey and the Tennessee distilling industry are going through a major revolution. Under a state law enacted in 2009, craft distilling was allowed in Tennessee for the first time in almost a hundred years. Up to that time, there were only three commercial distilleries in business—Jack Daniel's, George Dickel, and Prichard's (the up-start of the three, founded in 1997). Since 2009, Tennessee has granted more than a hundred DSP (distilled spirits plant) licenses, with more than forty distilleries now active in the state.

Tennessee is home to one of the most vibrant distilling industries in America, and is the second largest producing whiskey state in the nation. There are more than twenty new Tennes-see whiskey labels on the market, and that number is growing. What is fascinating is that they are all of good quality, and all distinct. Everyone expects every iteration of Tennessee whiskey to taste exactly the same. But why would they? Like any other region, there's great variety—some are big and robust, others are medium bodied with long flavors, and some drink smooth as silk. Variety is everything in this exciting new world.

TENNESSEE WHISKEY 101

The Lincoln County Process is what separates Tennessee whiskey from Kentucky bourbon. As they say at Jack Daniel's, bourbon comes out of the still, but Tennessee whiskey goes into the barrel. All whiskey carrying the moniker of "Tennessee whiskey"—with the exception of Prichard's, which was grandfathered in—is made using this process.

In most cases, the whiskey is made in the same way as most bourbons. The mash is cooked, yeast is added, the distiller's beer is poured down the still, and what emerges is essentially the same spirit. The only difference is that Tennessee whiskey must be passed through a charcoal filter before it is barreled. This filtering, this "mellowing process," is the Lincoln County Process.

There seems to be a lot of controversy about the process's history. The one fact we know for sure is that the practice was introduced to commercial whiskey making by a former enslaved man, Nathan "Nearest" Green. It is posited that he likely learned the technique from another slave. Green perfected his version of this process at Jack Daniel's.

"Although the process is very old, the term 'Lincoln County Process' is of recent coinage ... most people just called the practice 'leaching' or 'charcoal leaching,'" wrote whiskey historian Chuck Cowdery. "In the 19th century, it was common among Tennessee distillers to run their new make through sugar maple charcoal. For roughly the first half of that century, most whiskey was sold unaged, but improving the flavor of new make continued to seem like a good idea even after aging became the rule."

By the 1950s, the only distillery in America still leaching was Jack Daniel's. The folks in marketing wanted to brag on this extra step (you go and try to sell "leaching"!). They came up with a name they thought they could sell—the Lincoln County Process.

"The history of charcoal or char/fire for purity and filtration goes back thousands of years," says Chris Fletcher, Jack Daniel's master distiller. "We don't know who first applied it to spirits, but we know it was likely done in Kentucky and the Northeast prior to ever making its way down to Tennessee. The process of using charcoal to mellow spirits is part of how Green taught Jack Daniel to make whiskey. It's how Jack's family taught my grandfather to make whiskey, and it's how we keep making it today." Credit to Green.

The degree to which the spirit is exposed to the charcoal beds varies greatly. Jack Daniel's puts their spirit through eighty massive 14-foot-high tanks. George Dickel uses 13-foot-high tanks. In contrast, some distilleries pass the distillate through fish tank–sized charcoal filters. There is no regulation regarding the size of the filters but there is the legal insistence that the process be followed. Jack Daniel's burns $1 million worth of maple each year for the charcoal used in their filtration, and employs its own small fire department to keep up with the manufacturing demand.

"The beauty of Tennessee whiskey is that, while this process is required, each distiller is allowed the latitude to customize the variables to their own liking," said Andy Nelson, head distiller/co-owner of Nelson's Green Brier Distillery. "For example, someone may use much finer charcoal pieces or even much larger chunks than we do. Some may allow the distillate to sit in the vat for much longer, perhaps even soak for a bit as opposed to showering through, and some may utilize a much taller or shorter vat than we do."

Old Dominick Distillery does not have the large tanks of charcoal that Jack Daniel's does. Master distiller Alex Castle's whiskey goes through a smaller cylinder of charcoal. "Every time I point to our charcoal filter, I say, 'That is a Kentucky girl's version, or concept, of Tennessee whiskey.'" She laughs. "That is what you get when you ask someone who's been trained in the Kentucky bourbon world. I make Tennessee whiskey."

When asked if she was a Tennessee whiskey believer and if she tasted the difference before and after the Lincoln County Process, Castle responded, "I do not taste the difference in ours. I use so little charcoal. I am a traditionalist when it comes to bourbon. I try to use the charcoal so it is not an additive. Or a distraction. I don't want to do any of that. Am I a believer? Absolutely. I think that's what is great about the category. You can kind of treat it how you want to, so it can impact the whiskey, or it doesn't have to."

"There have been many names used to describe it, but 'mellowing' really fits the description because of how the whiskey tastes once it's allowed to drip through the charcoal," says Chris Fletcher at Jack Daniel's. This is the aha moment for many distillers who've since encountered the process.

"I am a huge believer in the Lincoln County Process," says Jim Massey of Fugitive Spirits. A famous distiller came to him with their very first bottles of bourbon. "'Look, Jim, this is really good bourbon we're getting out of Indiana. Why don't you come in with us, or just buy with us, and just start your brand that way?' No, I wanted to make whiskey out of Tennessee grain, because Tennessee whiskey ought to be from the good earth of Tennessee. I want to make a true

Tennessee whiskey." Massey uses heritage grains locally grown to make his whiskey, which he runs through maple charcoal.

Many people describe Tennessee whiskey as seeming smoother. Does this extra step somehow bring it closer to Irish whiskey, which is usually triple distilled? I asked Nicole Austin of George Dickel/Cascade Hollow Distilling, who had come to Dickel after making whiskey in Ireland. "I think that's a lot of people's misconception about Tennessee whiskey. If you're a nice person, it's a 'smoother version.' But I think that's some people being dismissive, they'd also be like, it's 'more boring' or 'less interesting,'" replied Austin. "I think there's this perception that you took this bourbon, which was perfect, and then you took out some things. . . .I think it actually allows you to access sometimes deeper, bigger, bolder flavors because you're not married to relative volatility as your only separation. It's a different tool. In Irish whiskey they are still using the same tool. It's distillation. Whereas with bourbon to Tennessee whiskey we're introducing a completely different methodology of separation based on affinity for activated carbon. Which is a totally different way in that it can be used that way to produce a lighter style, but it can also be used to produce a bolder, heavier style that is not burdened by undesirable characteristics.

"What I was struggling with sometimes when I was coming over to Dickel, I had the same understanding . . . that it was going to be a lighter style. Cascade/Dickel had all these taglines like 'Mellow as Moonlight,' and I had a really hard time squaring that with what I was seeing in the mature whiskey. Our Bottled in Bond is a massive whiskey. It's a big whiskey."

Nelson's Green Brier Distillery does it a little differently than Daniel's and Dickel. "We've built our 'mellowing tank' out of a whiskey barrel, so it measures approximately three feet tall by two feet wide at the belly," explained Andy Nelson. "We have removed both heads of the barrel and placed a stainless steel mesh screen about eight to twelve inches from the bottom with a piece of wool fabric on top of the screen. We then pack the barrel to just below the brim with fairly large chunks, some as large as the size of a softball, of sugar maple charcoal." A shower head–like mechanism is positioned just above the charcoal.

"After a distillation run, we place the barrel on top of a stainless steel tank and pump fresh distillate into the shower head, where it rains down evenly through the approximately two feet of charcoal and into the collection tank below," Nelson continued. "One distillation run will take around 20 to 25 minutes to run through our mellowing process." The distillate is then ready to go into the barrel.

Collier and McKeel, made in Nashville, uses a method that pumps the whiskey (instead of using gravity) slowly through ten to thirteen feet of sugar maple charcoal made from trees cut by local sawmills.

"At Leiper's Fork we make our own sugar maple charcoal, with a local mill up the road that has foresters bringing local sugar maple," says Lee Kennedy, distiller/co-owner of Leiper's Fork Distillery. "They cut it in staves, they air-dry it. We burn that down into charcoal using whiskey off the still. We try to do everything here. We start from scratch. We do every part of the process. We grow our own local grain, and our charcoal is the same way too.

"The distillate goes through about four feet of charcoal and it takes about 36 hours for that to happen. We slow drip it. We get a little bit of difference in taste … prefiltration, post filtration," continues Kennedy. "Almost a little bit of smokiness comes off the charcoal, but it's not flavoring the whiskey. It's basically removing some of the heavier fusel oils; it's like a Brita filter for whiskey."

"I'm interested in where we'll net out, ten or twenty or thirty years from now as producers. We have the choice to use this tool to go in either direction," said Nicole Austin of George Dickel. "That's what I mean, I believe in social terroir. I think it will be interesting to see how the community comes together to decide which path we're going to walk down. And I think it could go either way. You can use it to make more of an Irish whiskey version of bourbon, or an Islay Scotch version of bourbon. You can use it to go light or you can use it to go bold."

When Alex Castle of Old Dominick was asked her thoughts about Tennessee being the equivalent of Islay, she responded, "To me, Tennessee whiskey is a bourbon. I love that! Because it's perfect. Everyone understands Scotch now. That there are many different ranges. They're so unique."

And that's the thing. Today's Tennessee whiskey isn't for dousing with Coca-Cola. These are sophisticated whiskies. You will be wowed by this new generation of bottlings. They are fantastic neat, or with an ice cube. Order them with ice back. Sip 'em. Savor 'em. Seriously, why play with these? OK, if you must, experience them in a Boulevardier, Paper Plane, or Revolver.

NOTABLE EXPRESSIONS

Jack Daniel's

Because of how ubiquitous Jack Daniel's has become, I think Americans can take the great brand somewhat for granted. But there are a lot of good people who work very hard to make Jack Daniel's that good and that consistent. It's a bigger job than most people realize.

When asked what he thought when he accepted the job, former Jack Daniel's master distiller Jeff Arnett laughed and said, "I had one thought: 'I hope I don't screw it up.'" He was joking but he was also dead serious. "The one thing you notice here, especially in Lynchburg, is that there are guys who have their fathers' jobs, and their grandfathers' jobs. ...This isn't a job. This is heritage. This is a point of pride. I have never worked at a place where the employees take it to heart like they do here. Here's what I'm talking about. Each day, a bunch of these guys come to work with a Jack Daniel's T-shirt on. When they go home, on a Friday, they take a shower, and put on a clean Jack Daniel's T-shirt, and then go out for the night. That's the kind of local pride I'm talking about. How many employees at other companies do that?

"We make the best-selling whiskey in the world. We work hard every day to make sure we have consistency and integrity. It's got to taste the way it did ten years ago. It's got to taste the same way tomorrow. We have to constantly keep evaluating at each point in the process. Are we doing it consistently? Could we improve the process without changing the flavor? Is there a way to improve or ensure the quality without changing the recipe or the flavor profile? Millions of people love Jack Daniel's around the world. Our job is to make sure that each time they pick up a bottle it tastes just the same as the last bottle. It's a generational thing. No one wants to be a part of the generation that messed this thing up. It's a big responsibility. Every day you make something. Make sure it's good."

Chris Fletcher is the current master distiller at Jack Daniel's. "I'm born and raised in Lynchburg, Tennessee. I'm a Tennessean through and through. I'm very proud of the whiskey that we make here in Tennessee. Anything that has to do with our process, how we make whiskey ... transparency, transparency, transparency. We make whiskey the way my grandfather made whiskey, the way they did in the 1950s when my grandfather (Frank Bobo, master distiller, 1966–1988) started working here ... And it's not just me. There's a lotta families that can trace their way back here. Nearest Green has three great-great-grandkids that still work here today. It's a pretty normal thing here in Lynchburg. We all kind of grow up here, born the same way. You're sort of connected in the same way. To this place. It makes this place pretty special for sure."

"Our distillery operates in the most traditional method I've seen," added Fletcher. "The possibilities are almost endless, we don't have to rely on outsourcing to create new-to-world offerings." And that is the truth. They have their own dedicated building where they burn local maple to make their charcoal. They have their own dedicated nursery at the Jack Daniel's Orchard to make sure they have enough renewable maple and oak for their barrels. Jack Daniel's is one of the most unique, forward-thinking companies in the liquor business. They did not get to where they are by accident.

Since ascending to the captain's chair, Fletcher has unleashed a world of innovation at Jack Daniel's, one new release after another. He is the right man for the right time, and he has done it with resounding success. However, when it comes to my admiration for Jack Daniel's (and it is immense), the whiskey I will pour, and recommend, is the Jack Daniel's Single Barrel Select. Aged four to seven years, the bottle is impressive. This is rich, deep, mellow Tennessee whiskey at its best. Caramel, toasted oak, a bit of dried fruit, baking spices, cocoa, leather, and a slight hint of banana. The finish is a little pepper with Christmas spices. Sip this one. With ice back or a few rocks. Don't water it down. But give it just enough chill and it will reward you.

George Dickel

George Dickel and Cascade Hollow Distilling Co. are legacy brands in Tennessee and go as far back as Jack Daniel's. It went dormant during Prohibition, and was revived in 1958. Dickel is the second-largest distiller of Tennessee whiskey in the state.

Nicole Austin is the distiller at George Dickel/Cascade Hollow. She is a wonder woman, and easily one of the most accomplished distillers in the world. She has made whiskey all around the United States and in Europe, as well. She was a breath of fresh air when she was brought to Dickel, which was a neat trick since she followed in the footsteps of John Lunn and Allisa Henley. Since then, she has released a slew of impressive whiskies that have immediately cast the Dickel name and legacy in a new light.

Most impressive among her accomplishments is the George Dickel Bottled in Bond, which was named Whiskey of the Year by *Whiskey Advocate* in 2019, the year of its first release. It has received stellar marks throughout the industry and numerous awards. It is a big, bold whiskey, with plenty of flavor to spare, one to be savored, for sure. The first two Bottled in Bonds were each eleven-year-old whiskies. All the releases have been more than ten years in age, and all have been outstanding.

Nelson's Green Brier Distillery

Charles Nelson emigrated from Germany to the U.S. with his family when he was fifteen years old. He grew up to become a local merchant, owning a general store where he sold meat, coffee, and whiskey among other sundries. Whiskey became such a good seller for him that he bought a small distillery in Greenbrier, Tennessee. He also bought the patents for new, improved distilling techniques in 1867. By 1885 Nelson's Green Brier was producing 380,000 gallons of spirits per year, while Jack Daniel's was producing 23,000 gallons in the same sales period. It remained one of the largest producers in Tennessee through 1910, the year before Prohibition took hold in Tennessee.

Today, this Tennessee heritage brand has been revived by Charlie and Andy Nelson, distant relations of the founder. With help from consultant and former Maker's Mark distiller Dave Pickerell and Constellation Brands, Nelson's Green Brier Tennessee Whiskey is now the third most popular Tennessee whiskey in the country, and enjoys almost national distribution. It is an exceptional whiskey. Nelson's Green Brier is packaged in almost the exact label as it was at the turn of the last century. And the whiskey inside is excellent.

Nelson's Green Brier Tennessee Sour Mash Whiskey originally released a mash bill of 70 percent corn, 16 percent wheat, and 14 percent malted barley when they poured their first experimental Nelson's 108 whiskey. Today they are more secretive about the mash bill. One can only assume the recipe is not far from that mark. They were and remain adamant that they were not following the wheat trend but rather staying true to the original family recipe. Aged in charred new American oak barrels, the whiskey is approximately four years old. This is one of the best Tennessee whiskies out there. Big nose up front of caramel, ripe apple, cereal, and dried fruit, with a creamy honey and vanilla finish. Absolutely outstanding stuff!

Uncle Nearest Premium Whiskey

Perhaps no new distillery's debut has received as much attention as that of Uncle Nearest and, it seems, deservedly so. The distillery is named for Nathan "Nearest" Green (c. 1820–c. 1890). A former slave, he taught Jack Daniel the distilling technique that would come to be known as the Lincoln County Process. Green was hired as the Jack Daniel's Distillery's first master distiller, making him the first African American master distiller on record in the United States. His contributions to whiskey were obscured by time, but have come to light and been celebrated over the last decade.

The idea behind Uncle Nearest Premium Whiskey is simple—to pay tribute to the man who invented Tennessee whiskey. Fawn Weaver, best-selling author and entrepreneur, learned of Green's story in 2016 while on vacation. Within a month, she was living in Lynchburg, and whiskey would never be the same.

"What was amazing when I first started in the whiskey business is that I didn't realize that this was the first American spirit ever to commemorate an African American. Ever. Can you imagine? We've been here 400 years, and ours is the very first," said Weaver. Even more revolutionary is the company's executive suite. Four incredible women are at the helm of Uncle Nearest, the first major American spirit brand to have an all-female leadership/exec team. Add to that the fact that Victoria Eady Butler, the first African American female master blender of a major spirit brand, has also been the most award-winning master blender of the last ten years.

Uncle Nearest started outsourcing whiskey, mostly from Tennessee, but they have been laying down as much whiskey as quickly as possible as they start providing their own stocks in a bottle. Originally the distillery offered three whiskies, but in 2022 it debuted a whole new lineup. Uncle Nearest Single Barrel Premium Whiskey is the barrel strength of the classic original whiskey. Dark amber in color, it has notes on the nose of caramel, maple, shortbread biscuit, dark fruit, and vanilla, all of which come across on the palate. This is a fascinating, light-to-medium whiskey with flavor that lingers a good long time. And it's super smooth. You're gonna like this one.

A FEW MORE TO CONSIDER

Some of my other favorites from Tennessee include Clayton James Tennessee Whiskey (smooth and easy), Davidson Reserve Tennessee Whiskey (master distiller Carter Collins' chewy whiskey is filled with grain; complex, exceptional), Chattanooga Whiskey (one of the best distillers in the state—all malted grain), Old Dominick (Alex Castle is making intense, bold, beautiful whiskey under a recently revived heritage brand), Old Glory Distilling Co. (fantastic whiskey from distiller Matt Cunningham), and Leiper's Fork Distillery (elegant Bottled in Bond; the Highlands' single malt of Tennessee whiskey).

CANADIAN WHISKY

have a special fondness for Canadian whisky. When I was younger, the most interesting two bottles of whiskey in my father's liquor cabinet, as far as I was concerned, were Chivas Regal and Crown Royal. They were very fancy, very expensive whiskies. I particularly loved the look of Crown Royal, in its purple velvet bag. And back in the 1980s, there was a famous ad of a broken bottle of Crown Royal on the ground, with the tagline: "Have you ever seen a grown man cry?" That ad made a huge impression on me, even though I had not tasted Crown Royal at that point.

Now, in my later years, I have a very good friend, Shawn, who mans the bar at La Conca D'oro, a great little red sauce Italian restaurant in Catskill, New York, that he and his partner, Cheryl, run. Pictures of Shawn and Cheryl with Billy Joel and Mike Tyson are on the walls. What an unlikely place to discover Canadian whisky. Shawn was born and raised in the Detroit area. He roots for any team there that will make a run toward the playoffs. He's got a deep bass voice, shaggy hair, and a bushy beard, and wears a different Hawaiian shirt every night, no matter the season. His cedar-paneled bar is festooned with liquor bottles, Christmas lights year-round, and two televisions that play *Jeopardy* and *Wheel of Fortune* until the next sporting event comes on.

All the locals, including me, love to eat at the bar. The food is good and hearty. The laughs flow as much as the booze. Shawn is outspoken, funny, uses lots of colorful language, and most importantly, he's as authentic a person as I know. What you see is what you get. He's no-holds-barred. He is a showman and a circus master all in one. He knows how to handle people and keep them coming back.

And at the end of such nights, those locals who love to eat at the bar will buy Shawn a shot or a drink to thank him for his good company.

Because of the Detroit connection, Shawn is a big fan of Canadian whisky, and when you buy Shawn a drink, nine times out of ten that is what he will choose. His favorite is Canadian Club Reserve 9 Year Old. In Shawn's opinion, it is one of the best buys among the brown spirits, and that is saying something, as Shawn carries a lot of whisky.

CANADIAN WHISKY 101

"For too many people, the perception of Canada is of a milquetoast nation of polite and somewhat bland citizens," Canadian spirits journalist Christine Sismondo has written. "Unfortunately, that trope has long applied all too easily to our whisky, as well." Despite this wonderful bit of self-deprecation, Canadian whisky has never been hotter. There are actually quite a number of excellent whiskies in Canada. But the idea of whisky from Canada, to Americans, is confusing.

"I think we've been apologizing for it too long, and haven't gone out to tell our story," says Don Livermore, the master blender at the Hiram Walker & Sons Distillery in Windsor, Ontario. "Canadians have been doing themselves a disservice for eighty years."

"Canadian rye is one of the best-selling whiskies in America, and one of the least understood. Where information is sparse, myth has proliferated to fill in the blanks, leading to many strongly held misconceptions. So, let's explain the biggest myth right away: Most Canadian rye whisky contains a lot less than 51 percent rye grain. So why is it called 'rye'?" writes Davin de Kergommeaux, the dean of Canadian whisky writers.

"At the encouragement of Dutch and German immigrants who remembered spicy rye schnapps from home, distillers began adding small amounts of rye grain to their wheat mashes to improve the flavor of their otherwise bland (but fiery) whiskies. This new whisky style, with as little as 5 percent rye grain in the mash, was an instant success. So when people came to the mill to buy whisky, they would specify that they wanted the 'rye,'" de Kergommeaux explains. "Although the actual rye grain content rarely crept above 15 percent, these small amounts of rye so distinguished the new style that the name stuck, and the word 'rye' entered the Canadian lexicon as a synonym for whisky. Today, corn has largely replaced wheat in Canadian rye, but the use of judicious amounts of rye grain as flavoring persists."

"In Canada, spirits labeled 'rye' don't need to contain whisky made from rye grain, a hangover from our homegrown tradition—almost as old as the country itself—of blending wheat, corn, or barley spirits with rye distillate to give it a little spicy kick," agrees Sismondo. "Canada was actually the first country in the world to mandate minimum aging requirements in 1890—that the alcohol had to sit for a minimum of two years in wood."

As de Kergommeaux explains, "In America, the idea that rye whisky must contain at least 51 percent rye grain is so pervasive that many people are certain that whisky containing less than that is not real rye. For sure, it is not real *American* rye, but foreign distillers, including Canada's, are bound by the laws of their own countries, not America's. With the exception of Seagram's, which was located in a German Canadian community and sold some 100 percent rye-grain whisky, Canadian distillers rarely bottled whisky made with more than a small amount of rye."

In other words, a Canadian master blender in a ten-gallon batch might combine eight gallons of corn whisky and one gallon each of malted barley whisky and rye whisky, and they could call it rye whisky in Canada. It is more about flavor than content. In some cases, there are "Canadian whiskies" that contain much more rye than some whiskies on the market labeled "rye whisky," but they are not required to call it rye whisky. "Most Canadian whisky is majority corn … double column distilled," says Dave Mitton, Canadian whisky brand ambassador. "Then you'll take a one-column distilled rye and blend it in, usually less than 5 percent."

According to world whisky expert Simon Difford, "Blending is the key to Canadian whisky. It is produced from a wide range of grains: corn is by far the most important, while rye contributes the most flavor. As a rule, the more spice you smell in a Canadian whisky, the more rye is in the blend."

All this said, Canada has a rich and proud history of distilling. An example is Gooderham & Worts, once one of the largest distillers in Canada. In 1988, its former distillery complex was designated a National Historic Site of Canada. Today it has been revived as a combined office and residential living space, and comprises an entire district of Toronto.

One of the first bottles I bought when I got into whisky back in the 1990s was a bottle of Crown Royal. Crown Royal and Canadian Club are both blended whiskies. A bottle of Crown Royal might contain fifty different whiskies in its blend. I was so proud to have that purple velvet bag with its gold cord in my liquor cabinet.

I went on to discover bourbon, Scotch, and rye but Shawn brought me back to Canadian whisky. Smooth and easy to drink, many of the blended Canadian whiskies, like Canadian Mist, Seagram's V.O., Black Velvet, Rich & Rare, and Windsor Canadian, are great mixers, perfect for whisky and soda and whisky sours. And you really ought to try a Raymond Massey, named for the Canadian silver screen star, a mixture of whisky and ginger syrup, shaken, not stirred. It's strained into a highball glass, topped with sparkling wine, and usually gets a lemon peel garnish. That's an old timey Canadian cocktail.

Many folks have been drinking Canadian whisky without knowing it. Several American labels are bottled Canadian whisky, like Pendleton, Masterson's, Legacy, Lock Stock & Barrel, and, for many years, WhistlePig.

Today there are many very good Canadian blended whiskies available, and the craft scene keeps producing more, forcing the big boys to up their game. Superstar mixologists, especially Dave Mitton and Christine Sismondo, and geek distillers like Don Livermore, Martin Laberge, Don DiMonte, and Caitlin Quinn have made Canadian spirits super cool. There are so many unique offerings from producers like Eau Claire Distillery, Hansen Distillery, The Liberty Distillery, Odd Society Spirits, Resurrection Spirits, Dillon's Small Batch Distillers, Last Straw Distillery, Shelter Point Distillery, Sheringham Distillery, Stillhead Distillery, and many more.

While the Canadian whiskies of the past may have been considered mixers, many of these deserve to be sipped and savored. This isn't the Canadian whisky of the sixties and seventies, though I'm sure Shawn would fight you for it. It's never been cooler to sip Canadian whisky.

NOTABLE EXPRESSIONS
Crown Royal

Crown Royal is one of the most storied whiskies in North America, and it enjoys a solid reputation around the world. It was first introduced in 1939 by Samuel Bronfman for the 1939 royal tour of Canada by King George VI and his wife, Queen Elizabeth.

Bronfman set out to craft a whisky suitable for the royal couple. Legend has it that he trialed more than 600 blends. The whisky he presented to the king and queen, in a cut-glass decanter robed in a royal purple bag with gold stitching, was an exquisitely smooth blend of about fifty whiskies. The whisky was an instant hit, though it was sold only in Canada until the 1960s, when it was finally introduced to international markets. With its iconic purple bag, this enduring brand is the top-selling Canadian whisky in the United States, and the fourth best-selling whisky in the entire world.

Classic Crown Royal is a smooth, light whisky with wonderful complexity and terrific taste. Easy to sip, good on ice, and lovely in a cocktail. It's as good as it ever was. Crown Royal also releases other expressions, including Crown Royal Reserve, Crown Royal Black (aged in charred barrels and bottled at 90 proof), Blender's Mash (formerly Bourbon Mash), Fine De Luxe, and a host of popular flavors.

My favorite is Crown Royal Northern Harvest Rye, which is a 90 percent rye whisky. For those who like a punch-in-the-face rye, this is not your whisky. But if you like a rye that is smooth, complex, layered, and has subtle hints of vanilla and caramel, look no further. This whisky has won a pirate's chest full of medals. It was the first Canadian whisky to be anointed World Whisky of the Year (in 2016) in *Jim Murray's Whisky Bible*. "Technically speaking, Crown Royal Northern Harvest wouldn't qualify as a straight rye, since it's only 90 percent rye distillate. But that's still a whole lot more rye than most and the sharp qualities of rye shine through and add dimension to this rich and full blend," opined Christine Sismondo.

As American spirits journalist Margarett Waterbury writes, "This is an exceptionally fruit-forward rye more closely aligned with bourbon than funky, earthy American rye. The entire experience, from nose to finish, is clean, bright, and unmuddled. It's quite sweet, but the sweetness is balanced by a soft, grainy bitterness throughout that prevents the spirit from straying into syrupiness. A fun, bold sipping whisky for an affordable price." A surprising and lovely whisky.

Alberta Premium

"It wasn't too long ago that, in the eyes of most of the world, Canadian distilling was, to be quite honest, a bit of a joke. Not that many Canadians were aware of this fact, as we sipped proudly away on our rye whiskies, blissfully unaware of how precious little of their namesake grain they contained," wrote author Stephen Beaumont. "Alberta Spirits ... owned the 100 percent rye whisky category for many years with its Alberta Premium, a whisky that won international acclaim year after year. Many eventually followed Alberta Premium's lead, but it took some time for other distillers to catch on to the promise of Canadian rye."

Alberta Premium is still a damn good whisky, and a real rye in the eyes of Americans, since its mash bill is 100 percent Canadian rye. My favorite is Alberta Premium Cask Strength Rye. Big, bold flavor, with a nice punch. It's great neat, with a few drops of water, a rock, or on the rocks. This whisky stands up. And it stands tall in a cocktail too.

Lot No. 40 Canadian Rye Whisky

Possibly Canada's most famous 100 percent rye whisky, this has long been the darling of rye aficionados. Few whiskies in Canada have received more press than this bottle. Mike Booth, master distiller at Hiram Walker & Sons at the time, in doing some research into his family history, discovered a distant relation, one Joshua Booth, who had fought for the British during the American Revolution. After the war, Booth settled in Canada and became a distiller. "He was quite a successful businessman. He owned about seven gristmills, one of them located on a plot of land—Lot 40," said Booth. That Lot 40 was the inspiration for the brand, which launched in 1998.

Dr. Don Livermore, Hiram Walker's master distiller now for nearly thirty years, once said about its distillation process, "It's 100 percent rye whisky. The rye is passed once through a column still and then a pot still . . . When you put that fermented rye mash once through the column still you keep the grain character (spicy), as well as the floral, the fruity notes."

Lot No. 40 100% Pot Still Rye Whisky is crafted in small batches using 100 percent rye grain in a single copper pot still. This concentrates the spicy rye notes, while retaining the fruity and floral notes from fermentation. The whisky is then aged in virgin white oak barrels to bring forth notes of vanilla, caramel, and toffee. Nice doses of rye spices and white pepper, a lovely nuttiness, and a soft sweetness of brown sugar. "Full bodied and rich," wrote Stephen Beaumont, "sufficiently spicy for a Manhattan; with a complexity suited to solitary sipping on its own or with ice." I love the Cask Strength and the Lot 40 Dark Oak (my favorite), the latter of which was named World's Best Rye at the 2021 World Whisky Awards.

Last Straw

Last Straw Distillery is owned by distilling rebel and groundbreaker Don DiMonte, who founded it in 2013 in Vaughan, Ontario, though it did not open until 2016, as he fought antiquated Canadian liquor laws. He is a hero in the region for this crusade. "Don't think he was just pushing paper for those three years, Don has been working with all the local distillers. Helping them where he can and in turn getting help and advice from them," wrote Kole McRae, of the website Toronto Boozehound. DiMonte is known as an innovator, willing to try almost anything once. DiMonte's Last Straw Straight Ontario Rye is made from 100 percent Ontario rye grain, sourced from community-based mills that buy primarily from small organic family farms in the area. It is aged for three years in new no. 3 char American oak casks.

Davin de Kergommeaux describes this whisky as having "aromas of sweet toffees, blackstrap, sweet spices, fresh artist's oil paint, dust, and candied fruit mingle on a very aromatic nose. Bold, brash, and loud on first sip, Cask 2 Rye then settles into a vibrant yet simply lovely whisky." It is also sometimes available in Cask Strength. One of the most sought-after craft rye whiskies in all of Canada and rightly so.

Sheringham Distillery

Sheringham Distillery is owned and operated by Jason and Alayne MacIsaac, husband and wife juggernaut, in Sooke, British Columbia, on the west coast of Vancouver Island. They use time-honored distilling methods and 100 percent B.C.-grown grains to make their small batch handcrafted spirits, which have wowed critics, especially the Woodhaven Whiskeys #1 and #2 and the Red Fife Whiskey. Red Fife has a "spicy toffee nose, with background notes of appealing earthiness. On the palate, it has a fruity caramel front and more nutty, grainy midpalate, finishing with a flourish of spice," wrote Stephen Beaumont.

"Consistently awesome," said wine and spirits journalist Rémy Charest of Sheringham after judging at the Artisan Distillers Canada 2021 Spirits Awards. "I've been judging for four years. Sheringham rye is brilliant." Sheringham Small Batch Rye Whiskey has been aged for four years in new American oak, with a mash bill of rye, wheat, and malted barley. A full-bodied monster of a rye with lovely oak tones.

Sheringham's rye has become something of a unicorn, but then again, all of their whiskies are difficult to find, but definitely worth seeking! Promise.

Shelter Point Distillery

This is the kind of whisky distillers tell each other about. Established in 2011, Shelter Point Farm and Distillery is located on 380 acres in Oyster River, British Columbia, on the eastern side of Vancouver Island. Farmed for generations, Shelter Point is one of the last seaside farms on the island. The owner is Patrick Evans, a third-generation farmer whose family members were turn-of-the-twentieth-century pioneers in the Comox Valley. If you want good whisky, this is the place to come.

Shelter Point Single Cask Rye is a small-batch limited-release bottling that consists of only 150 to 200 hand-numbered bottles. The whisky is made from 100 percent rye and picks up influences of bourbon from the American oak cask and malt whisky from the aromas in their warehouse. Sweet, spicy, and complex, this whisky is a stunner. Available at the distillery only.

"Civilization begins with distillation"

—William Faulkner

RYE
WHISKEY

Rye whiskey is the highest expression of American whiskey there is. I didn't come up wih that, and I don't know who the first person is who did. I can only confirm that many people in the business feel this way. Rye is the stepping stone from bourbon to single-malt whiskey.

In 2006, 2007, and 2008 I grew rye on my farm, the Hudson-Chatham Winery, in the northern Hudson Valley. My single purpose was to sell it to Ralph Erenzo, the owner/distiller of Tuthilltown Distillery, located across the river, at the foot of the Shawangunk Mountains, who was just starting to make rye whiskey. He was one of the people responsible for bringing rye back to its former popularity. I knew enough to know that what was happening on the whiskey scene was possibly historic. I was new to farming. Inexperienced. Made lots of mistakes. But I loved it.

There is nothing more exciting, nothing more beautiful to grow, than rye grain. You plant it in the fall, a cover crop for the winter. It sprouts relatively quickly, but during the coldest of the winter months in this climate it goes into a kind of hibernation, no higher than an inch tall. Then, suddenly, it seems to grow before your eyes once the vernal equinox hits.

Watching the four or five acres of grain we had planted slowly sway in the crystal blue spring afternoons was like watching the ocean. It was a stunning green-blue, and it rippled like water on the hillside, affected by even the slightest breeze. It was the most mesmerizing thing I have ever seen. And every person I talked to about it thought I was nuts until I dragged them out there to watch it themselves. Then they too were captivated.

Once the rye was cut and threshed, I called Ralph. He asked me if we had harvested it by combine, if we had filtered it. I had no idea what he was talking about. A local farmer had done it for me, and he had taken the long grass for his Angus. I was left with bins of seeds. How did I know whether or not there were any other high grasses mixed in there? You need to filter it, he told me, requiring a screen and a contraption I did not have. It was a big mistake on my part. I shrugged. We would grow the grain again the next year.

As it was, I became too wrapped up in my own business, making and selling wine, and left the grain business to others who knew what they were doing. I continued planting it as a cover crop (which I needed), and I was satisfied, watching the waves and swirls of the grain on sunny days. It even sounded like water lapping on the shore. I never got tired of it.

My cash crop was grapes. And during the three years we'd been growing the rye, the local deer had been having their babies in our back fields. When it came time to crop our 2009 vintage, the deer decimated our vineyards in a matter of days. There would be no estate wine that season. A wine consultant insisted that we had to raise the height of our fence, and we had to stop growing rye. Immediately. And that was the end of my attempt to grow rye at the farm. In the end, we grew a lot more grapes, which, it turns out, we were a lot better at.

So I bought my Tuthilltown rye at the store, just like everyone else. By then, I was editing a slew of whiskey and cocktail books at my day job, where I worked with *Esquire*, Salvatore Calabrese, Clay Risen, and an exceptional mixologist named Jim Meehan, who owned the celebrated Please Don't Tell speakeasy in New York City's East Village. We published his book *The PDT Cocktail Book* in 2011. By then I knew a half dozen well-known mixologists, and we were all knee-deep in the new cocktail culture.

Rye was not new to me. My father had been a dry whiskey guy. He didn't like bourbon at all: "Too sweet!" he would grimace. He favored a Manhattan made with rye—that was as sweet a drink as he could stomach.

Either it was rye, with one ice cube or a splash of water in it (Old Overholt or Rittenhouse—"Pennsylvania" real rye in his eyes—having come from New Jersey and having been a fan of Philadelphia restaurants), or Scotch.

Rye whiskey made a run starting in the 2000s like few types of spirits anyone has ever seen. And most of the industry was caught flat-footed. The biggest, most bullish of rye's boosters was Dave Pickerell, master distiller at Maker's Mark for more than fourteen years. By the time I met him, in 2012, Dave was already the supernova star of brown spirits, and particularly rye. Everyone watched him, somewhat unsure if his unshakable faith in rye was true religion or misplaced zealotry.

"First of all, I love history, and rye whiskey is inextricably tied to early American history. It was being made—and made well—for more than a century before bourbon was created," Dave told the Robb Report. "Second, I love the character of rye whiskey, especially Monongahela rye (rye whiskey with no corn in the mash bill). It can be bold and spicy, full-bodied, and versatile. And most classic American whiskey cocktails were originally created using rye."

It is important to note, as Dave did, that rye whiskey predates bourbon. Rye originated when farmers needed to do something with the rye grain left over from the previous season. In that time, it was not as easy to store grain without it going bad. The grain could be converted to distiller's beer, then whiskey, and was easier to store, transport, and use for bartering or sale. In the late 1790s, George Washington ran the largest distillery in America, and a large portion of what he produced was rye. Old Overholt, the nation's oldest continuously running rye whiskey brand, was founded in 1810.

I remember talking to Pickerell about the new rye venture he had taken on, to be called WhistlePig, saying, in shock, that I knew rye was rising, but was he really willing to bet that much money on only rye? No other whiskey in the portfolio? Wasn't that taking an awful chance with someone else's millions? He looked me dead in the eye, as if I were a child. Yes. Rye was going to be the next big thing. I remember thinking, *He has forgotten more about whiskey than I know, but it still seems a little crazy*. Boy, what a bag of hammers I was.

Pickerell explained his reasoning: "We do have aspirations of being America's grown-up, go-to whiskey. What I mean by that is when people who are drinking bourbon start looking for something with more character, we want to be there for them as an alternative to Scotch." This was coming from a man who'd made Maker's Mark for more than a decade.

And that is exactly what rye is, and has become. It's the next step after you've satisfied your sweet tooth with bourbon, and you're ready for a more grown-up whiskey. It's kind of like learning to drink sweet white wine, then wanting to graduate to chardonnay and eventually cabernet sauvignon, or liking light pilsners and eventually moving onto IPAs.

When the rye craze first hit, not a lot of it was out there. Only a half dozen old rye labels had survived Prohibition and the rise of clear spirits (gin, vodka, and tequila). When the pendulum swung back, many major producers were caught off guard. Large stocks were bought up like they were gold. Sleuthing through warehouses for extant barrels of rye was the height of craft whiskey skullduggery. Even some of the newest, hippest labels were, at first, blended from stocks procured in Indiana and Canada.

RYE WHISKEY 101

For it to be rye whiskey, rye must make up at least 51 percent of the mash bill. Some brands have much more that 51 percent, others do not. There are lighter, sweeter ryes, made with a substantial amount of corn, and then there are the high-rye whiskies, with 80 percent or more rye.

Rye was why cocktails were invented. The original Old Fashioned and Manhattan were both made only with rye. The bourbon variations came later. The spice of rye holds its own with other ingredients. Internationally known Canadian mixologist Dave Mitton advises to use rye as well. And many mixologists, like famed Dale DeGroff, recommend using a 90 proof whiskey or better in a cocktail, so that the whiskey does not get lost.

"I like rye for cocktails because it is unrepentantly what it is," says Connecticut bartender-at-large Geoffrey Smith. "It's the lead singer and everyone else in the band better recognize that."

Whiskey ambassador Daniella Solano is unequivocal: "Personally, I believe every Manhattan should be made with rye."

"When my career in the beverage industry began in the early 2000s," wrote spirits journalist and cocktail book author Amanda Schuster, "I was primarily a single malt Scotch drinker, but it was rye whiskey, not bourbon (yet), that sparked my interest in American whiskies. It turns out I wasn't alone. By 2007, when I was the Assistant Spirits Buyer at Astor Wine & Spirits in New York City, rye's hipness was such that we couldn't keep the stuff, any of the stuff, on the shelves for more than a day or two. In 2020 it's hard to imagine a time when there wasn't enough rye to go around. Rye whiskey of all shapes, sizes, colors, and provenance are elbowing each other for shelf space these days, and the category continues to evolve." When Schuster started, there were small quantities of old legacy brands—Old Overholt, Pikeville, Rittenhouse, Jim Beam, and Wild Turkey. Today, we are at the zenith of American rye whiskey. Even in Scotland there are new ryes being born.

In the U.S., there are many styles and categories of rye, such as Maryland (sweeter) and Pennsylvania ryes (more robust), Empire ryes (the entire product grown, malted, and distilled in New York State), single malt ryes, heirloom ryes, and hybrid ryes (triticales).

One of my favorite rye whiskies is also one of the most unique in the world—Old Potrero. I discovered it when I was working in Philadelphia, around the time Michael Jackson was first promoting single malts. I bought it because it was a single malt—I only realized it was made from rye (not barley) after I brought it home. Chagrined, I opened the bottle anyway. That whiskey was eye opening.

Old Potrero Single Malt Straight Rye Whiskey was originally released in 1996 as part of Fritz Maytag's Anchor Distilling Company, which he founded in 1993. It is now a part of Hotaling & Co. Distilling. This was one of the first big ryes made in America. Their goal was to position the product as a single malt whiskey. With the mad rush for marketing rye, they repositioned the product slightly without changing the actual liquid that went inside the bottle. The mash bill is 100 percent malted rye (hence the single malt designation). Stone fruit and a certain cognac feeling come through. A fine sipper but I must admit I love it in a Manhattan. This is one of the most sophisticated ryes made in America. Neat, one rock, with a drop of water—this is tremendous whiskey.

PENNSYLVANIA VS. MARYLAND RYE

Pennsylvania-style rye has a high rye content—a drier, spicier, bolder rye. Maryland contains corn (the amount can vary, with rye always being 51 percent of the mash bill) and, as a result, is slightly sweeter, with more fruit and caramel, and a hint of spice.

However, spirits historians in general tend to challenge that there ever was a Maryland, or Baltimore, rye. Some opine that there was more rectification than distilling going on in Maryland. "Historically, rectification was the process of redistilling whiskey to strip out some or all of the whiskey flavor elements," whiskey expert Chuck Cowdery explained. "A rectifier mixes a little straight whiskey (e.g., straight bourbon) with a much larger percentage of grain neutral spirits (whiskey made from a number of grains), plus flavoring and coloring, to produce blended whiskey."

According to spirits historian Michael Veach, Maryland rye was originally a rectified rye that used flavoring agents. Veach believes that additives "such as prune juice, cherry juice, caramel coloring, and other ingredients" were included to create flavor and stylistic differences among brands. "Many Maryland ryes were so highly rectified that when the Pure Food and Drug Act was enacted in 1906, they simply quit making them rather than admit what was in the whiskey. These whiskies probably ranged in quality as did most rectified whiskies. The best were probably made by marrying straight rye whiskies and pure ingredients like Port or some other fortified wine and fruit juices. They must have been popular for the style to grow outside of Maryland."

Before 1909 the term "Maryland Rye" was used to denote a softer style of rye. But many ryes that bore the moniker, e.g., Maryland Union Club

Rye, Old Maryland, and My Maryland Rye, were actually distilled elsewhere, in this case, respectively, in New York City, St. Louis, and Cincinnati. So, less scrupulous distillers blatantly appropriated a regional identifier (which is no longer allowable). "And what's a little product confusion among friends anyway?" as Chuck Cowdery pointed out. According to him, it was a marketing ploy.

NOTABLE EXPRESSIONS

Dad's Hat Pennsylvania Rye Whiskey

The distillery for Dad's Hat is located in a restored old factory and has a feel that is something between a mill and a Hollywood backlot. Co-founders Herman C. Mihalich and John S. Cooper have known each other since they were fraternity brothers in 1976. I went there because, despite the quirky brand name, this is one of the most important producers of quality rye whiskey in America. They make rye whiskey and that is all they do. And they make an old-fashioned high-rye content rye—one that is big, like a punch in the mouth, just like it should be, about halfway between Philadelphia and Trenton. This is East Coast whiskey. This is John O'Hara, no soda water, no sermons. A flavorful rye whiskey like from the good old days. So you lean back, and you enjoy the conversation a little longer because the whiskey is good and so is the show.

Dad's Hat does everything right. They use only rye and barley in their whiskies. Herman uses a traditional 500-gallon pot still with a modern side column. The rye is not only grown locally, it is a heritage variety, known as Rosen, that was popular in pre-Prohibition whiskies.

Dad's Hat Pennsylvania Straight Rye Whiskey Prohibition Style is distilled farm-to-bottle with locally harvested grain, and aged for a minimum of four years. A rich, full-flavored rye, with pine and toasty oak on the nose, all the classic notes are there. One helluva bottle. Brace yourself, this is big whiskey. Outstanding.

Sagamore Spirit

Sagamore Spirit is owned by Kevin Plank, the entrepreneur who founded Under Armour, also based in Baltimore. It gets its name from Sagamore Farm, famous in thoroughbred horse racing, which is also owned by Plank. Sagamore Spirit started in 2012 with longtime Seagram's master distiller Larry Ebersold (who made more rye whiskey than anyone else in America) overseeing development.

Sagamore distills two different mash bills and then combines them into one whiskey. Sagamore Spirit Straight Rye Whiskey is a high-rye with a mash bill of 95 percent rye and 5 percent malted barley; the second has a sweeter, softer mash bill of 52 percent rye, 43 percent corn, and 5 percent malted barley. The water for their spirits flows from a spring house built in 1909 at Sagamore Farm—naturally filtered spring water, fed from a limestone aquifer.

"We age them separately for four to seven years. Every product we have is a blend of those two straight ryes. It varies a little bit from product to product. It allows us to define our Maryland style. You want to get those classic rye spicy notes you expect, your clove, your cinnamon, your nutmeg. It allows us to achieve a balance that harmonizes well with the sweet, fruity floralness you get from barely legal rye, with stone fruit notes, etc.," says general manager Brian Treacy.

Sagamore Double Oak Rye Whiskey is whiskey that has been aged four to five years and then rebarreled into toasted new oak barrels for an additional eighteen months. The result is a big, deep rye, with tremendous flavor and complexity. Dark golden in color, its nose features orange zest, nutmeg, toffee and caramel, honey, and baking spices. Candied orange and Christmas spices arrive on the palate as promised. Brown sugar and vanilla and a hint of pepper linger nicely. A very drinkable, easy dram.

WhistlePig Whiskey

Certainly, one of the most memorable trips I ever took to a distillery was my visit to WhistlePig. It was February, and Vermont was covered in a picturesque blanket of snow, complete with barns and mountain roads. I went there with my companions Rich Srsich and John Crabtree (part of my Northeastern Research Team), and sat in its spacious tasting room with its staff and two magnificent fireplaces, each fully ablaze.

WhistlePig Whiskey is one of the premier producers of rye in North America. The farm is comprised of 500 acres in the foothills of the Green Mountains. And yes, it has live pigs (Orwell and Sisi). WhistlePig ryes have been nothing short of a stunning success.

This small distillery was conceived back in 2008 as a brand specializing in rye whiskey. Initially all the whiskey released was acquired from other producers in Indiana and Canada, and then further aged and blended in Vermont. In 2015 a still was built and fired. Now the farm produces its own rye, wheat, and barley. In 2017, WhistlePig released its first single estate Triple Terroir whiskey, FarmStock Rye Crop 001, following it up with Rye Crops 002 and 003 in 2018 and 2019. Triple Terroir refers to the three levels of terroir—the estate grain, the water, and the use of local Vermont oak in its barrels. The most recent release, HomeStock, is a blend of four-year-old 100 percent WhistlePig rye with five-year-old sourced barley and wheat whiskies.

WhistlePig is now led by two intrepid young women—Head of Whiskey Development, Liz Rhoades (a former brewer and Diageo veteran), and Chief Blender, Meghan Ireland (a chemical engineer and craft cider veteran), keep the ship headed in the right direction. They are the day-to-day operations managers, and they are impressive. There is a good combination of youth and experience guiding this company into the future.

I have always thought of WhistlePig Distillery as one of the most art-ful craft blended whiskey houses in the world, up there with Compass Box Whisky in Europe and a few others. But what is more exciting is to see a company that clearly knows how to blend and bottle world-class whiskey take the very careful steps necessary to become a world-class distillery. And that is what is happening.

WhistlePig 10 Year Old and FarmStock are great whiskies, as are its legendary The Boss Hog bottlings, and all are certainly worthy of your time. But I have to tell you that one of the most drinkable American ryes is, without a doubt, PiggyBack 100% Rye. This was the late Dave Pick-erell's last creation with the distillery before he passed away. In the sum-mer of 2018, Dave scoured the barrel houses with one mission in mind: to create a WhistlePig rye with that signature spiciness and robustness, but one that would be affordable for mixologists to use in cocktails. The goal was a mash bill of 100 percent rye. He created a rye aged not less than six years, with a hint of cinnamon, tangerine, grapefruit zest, and lemon oil, as well as vanilla and spice. A big shot of flavor and intensity, and eminently drinkable.

BLENDED SCOTCH WHISKY

Approximately 90 percent of all the Scotch consumed worldwide is blended whisky, and it was the only kind of Scotch available on the market until 1964. My father and his friends, who drank Scotch back in the day, were raised on blended whiskies. Johnnie Walker, Black & White, Cutty Sark, Ballantine, J&B, Dewar's, Haig Club, White Horse, Passport, and Grant's—classic old-style labels—were among the many brands they purchased. During the holidays, high-end blended Scotch brands like Chivas Regal and Pinch, which were aged twelve to fifteen years, also made their appearances. Scotch in America at that time was found in just two places—dive bars and country clubs.

Those were the Scotches I knew growing up. Those were the bottles in my father's liquor closet. If my parents had a party, those were the bottles on a temporary bar that towered like the New York skyline over an ice bucket, some lime and lemon wedges, and a few bottles of seltzer. My father and his friends, dressed in loud plaid sports jackets and colored shirts, would play the Rat Pack, The 5th Dimension, Herb Alpert, Tom Jones, Otis Redding, Johnny Hartman, and The Temptations on the stereo, and smoke up a storm, until the room was foggy with it, accompanied by the clink of cubes and the splash of whisky being poured.

For a kid, those were heady times, to watch a room full of grown-ups slowly finish the bottles, chatting away, munching on Ritz Crackers and cheddar cheese swirled with port. Our kitchen was classic seventies—avocado, burnt orange, and mustard yellow. As I grew older, I would be asked to make a drink or two. And so I was initiated slowly into the world of the adults. Lessons were taught about the difference between one, two, and three fingers of whisky. An ice cube versus rocks. A splash of soda. Who liked a lime, and who liked a lemon. I reveled in my new power, my new place in the adult world. Occasionally I would sip a drink, hoping to appreciate the finer points of Scotch, but it all tasted like dreck to me, especially the smoky ones—so much so that I worried that somehow someone's cigarette ashes had slipped into the glass. Ugh!

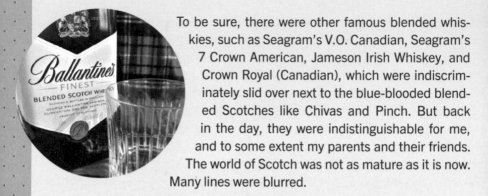

To be sure, there were other famous blended whiskies, such as Seagram's V.O. Canadian, Seagram's 7 Crown American, Jameson Irish Whiskey, and Crown Royal (Canadian), which were indiscriminately slid over next to the blue-blooded blended Scotches like Chivas and Pinch. But back in the day, they were indistinguishable for me, and to some extent my parents and their friends. The world of Scotch was not as mature as it is now. Many lines were blurred.

BLENDED SCOTCH WHISKY 101

The art of blending whiskies is a relatively recent one, given the long history of whisky itself. Andrew Usher introduced the concept of blending in Edinburgh in the 1860s. Up until then Scotch whisky was a local industry, sold in small quantities. These blends were much easier to drink, and soon a larger following outside of Scotland was established. As the industry increasingly adopted this style, the further the product spread, first to London and the surrounding environs, and then to the rest of the world.

Single malt Scotch was not introduced as a bottled whisky until 1964. Before that, every bottle that was sold to the public was blended. Blended Scotch is only made in Scotland, and these are some of the oldest whisky brands in the world. Each of the top ten best-selling Scotch blends has a long history chock-full of stories. Each one is almost a movie of its own.

Blended whiskies are just what you might imagine, a combination of different whiskies, blended to a flavor profile in such a way that it can be repeated again and again, over time. Most blended whiskies around the world are made in a similar fashion. There are few industry standards when it comes to blending. In most cases, a cellar master or blender chooses the whiskies, they are combined in large vats, and then they are redistributed into oak for a period so that the flavors can meld.

The main ingredient in any blend is a light whisky made from assorted grains. Usually it's dominated by wheat, but it can also contain barley, rye, corn, rice, and/or any number of grains. This mash is brewed into what is called a distiller's beer (no hops here!) and then distilled to create a smooth, light, clear spirit. This is called grain whisky, which has its own category.

This is then blended with other whiskies. Many of these are single malt whiskies from Scotland, some younger, some older. Some might have the sweet highlights of a Highland single malt or the peaty notes of an Islay to layer in a touch of smoke. The idea is to create a complex, well-balanced blend of flavors. Some blends contain as many as fifteen to twenty different whiskies.

Numerous blends carry an age statement. The age statement on a blend reflects the age of the youngest whisky in the blend. For instance, with Chivas Regal 25 Year Old, the youngest whisky in the blend is 25 years old. The aged whiskies are assembled and aged in neutral wood, and then moved to a second barrel, such as an ex-sherry cask, for finishing.

In the 1980s, The Famous Grouse, an old brand, was reintroduced. In recent years, newer whisky houses in Scotland brought to market an array of blended whiskies. The giants also embraced the trend, upgrading their packaging and releasing a slew of new whiskies. Changes were happening all over the place.

For a long time, the Scotch world was the domain of men, but in recent years that has begun to change, and nowhere more brightly than at

Johnnie Walker. When the long-venerated master blender Dr. Jim Beveridge, who had served the company well for years, announced his retirement in 2021, Diageo announced the appointment of Johnnie Walker's first-ever female master blender, Dr. Emma Walker, who took up the reins from Dr. Beveridge.

Blended whiskies are excellent in whisky cocktails—a classic Whisky Sour or Whisky Smash, a Rob Roy, or Rusty Nail. Because they are light-flavored whiskies, they are also very easy to drink with ice or soda. Add a slice of lemon or orange and you're off to a very nice time. Age statement bottles and blended single malts deserve more respect. Neat, with ice back, maybe a glass of water so you might put in a few drops. They are to be savored.

NOTABLE EXPRESSIONS

Shackleton Mackinlay's Rare Old Highland Malt Whisky

This is possibly the most meaningful bottle of whisky I have in my collection. It's a story on top of a story. I'd known John Whalen for more than twenty years. And together we had helped build a company that we didn't own. When that company was sold, we went our own ways. I built a winery; he built another publishing company. And he asked me to help him. It was one of the best things I ever did.

He had fought hard to establish his business. We worked hard. And when he made his first big year, he bought me a bottle of whisky as a thank you. I was astounded. He bought me this whisky. It was such a special bottle, all by itself, and it was even more so because he had gifted it to me.

I didn't even want to drink it. I kept it in my wine cellar and gazed at it from time to time. I was immensely proud of it, but also felt unworthy, thinking it was *way* beyond me, way beyond my contribution. Too nice a present for an idiot like me.

Sir Ernest Henry Shackleton's life is the stuff of legend; he is one of the most famous of the explorers of the Heroic Age of Antarctic Exploration. He led three British expeditions. His second expedition (1907–1909) set a new record for farthest south, only 97 geographical miles from the South Pole. As a result of this and other discoveries, he was knighted by King Edward VII. But he gained everlasting fame in 1917 when his ship *Endurance* was enveloped and crushed by pack ice, stranding his crew. Shackleton, in a desperate bid to save his men, sailed a rescue boat 720 nautical miles in rough seas, then trekked over a mountain range to a whaling station, where he chartered a boat to go back for his crew. Not a single man was lost. Shackleton died on January 5, 1922, during another expedition, and is buried in Antarctica.

During Shackleton's 1907 Antarctic expedition, he left behind cases of Mackinlay's Rare Old Highland Malt Whisky. In 2007, the whisky was discovered, frozen beneath their base camp. It was then that Whyte & Mackay attempted to re-create the whisky blend. So famous an event was this in the whisky world that there were television specials and even a book relating all the events that led to this unique whisky.

The recovered bottles were analyzed in the Invergordon lab, and recreated by Richard Paterson, the master blender of Whyte & Mackay, which now owns Mackinlay's. The whisky, the bottle, and even the packaging of the original were closely reproduced. This is a classic Highlands whisky, featuring cereal, vanilla, orange, lemon zest, and dried apple and pear, with notes of spice and ginger, butter, honey, and light brown sugar, and a slight hint of smoke. A special whisky, one that should be drunk with a copy of a Shackleton book in your lap or in a dark wood-paneled room festooned with library lamps and paintings of old clipper ships. Ice set back, neat. Maybe a cube halfway through. The conversation should be about nothing current, only important things, like memories, old friends, battles fought and won and fought and lost. Sometimes the losses are easier, sweeter to remember, knowing they have been overcome. Those are the conversations really old, close friends can answer for. Cheers.

The Dimple Pinch

Haig Whisky may be the oldest of all the Scotch whiskies, first distilled in 1824 by John Haig in the old Cameronbridge Distillery in Scotland. Haig Whisky rapidly grew to become one of the most successful and popular Scotch whiskies in the world. The distillery has changed hands numerous times, and now falls under the Diageo umbrella.

Haig Dimple Pinch is one of the shining stars of the Haig line. It carries a fifteen-year age statement and features a heavier malt influence due to the addition of whiskies from Glenkinchie and Linkwood. This is a lovely, understated whisky, light but with a terrific malt character. Toffee, caramel, butterscotch, hints of apple and pear. A fantastic whisky. This is a crowd pleaser and a bottle to impress with.

Johnnie Walker Blended Scotch Whisky

Without question, Johnnie Walker has been and remains, by far, the largest and best-selling brand of Scotch whisky in the world. The red, black, green, gold, and blue labels are legendary and iconic. And a slew of higher-end releases have secured its reputation even among the purists.

But did you ever wonder who Johnnie Walker actually was? John (Johnnie) Walker was born in 1805, near Kilmarnock in Ayrshire, Scotland.

In 1820, his father died and left him £417 in trust. That same year he invested in a warehouse, grocery, and wine and spirits shop on the High Street in Kilmarnock. He became a pillar of the community, involved in the local trade associations and Freemasons. Though he abstained from alcohol himself, by 1852 his own brand of blended whisky, Walker's Kilmarnock Whisky, was locally popular.

Eventually John's son Alexander, after apprenticing with tea merchants in Glasgow, returned to take over his father's business. He learned the art of blending at the teahouse and used that experience to blend whiskies to create Old Highland Whisky (eventually renamed Johnnie Walker Black Label), the blend that made Johnnie Walker famous. In the end, when Alexander was ready to hand the company off to *his* sons, 90 to 95 percent of its sales were from whisky.

Johnnie Walker Double Black, released in 2011, is one of my favorite blends. The iconic Johnnie Walker Black is a blend of about forty whiskies from around Scotland, including both smoky island single malts as well as sweeter Speyside and Highland malts. All the whisky is at least twelve years old. Double Black amplifies the bigger flavors, for a darker, smokier whisky. Double Black is matured in heavily charred oak casks. A little bigger, chewier, and in your face.

The Green Label 15 Years is the favorite Johnnie Walker of many whisky writers around the world. It is a sumptuous whisky, made with malts from the four corners of Scotland. The whisky conveys tremendous flavors with great balance. It is a perfect showcase for the many regions of Scotland. Lovely notes of apple, pear, fig, with rich notes of oak and caramel, a hint of cedar, and a peated finish that is incredibly well balanced.

Monkey Shoulder

Monkey Shoulder is made by William Grant & Sons, a family-owned distillery whose beginnings stretch back to 1887. Early in the 2000s William Grant saw an opportunity to create a Scotch whisky intended for mixed cocktails. The first bottle of the blend was called Batch 27. The brainchild of Brian Kinsman, Monkey Shoulder is a blend of malts from Kininvie, Balvenie, and Glenfiddich. Technically, Monkey Shoulder could be referred to as a triple malt but it is sold as a blended malt Scotch whisky, and was the first of its kind. Monkey Shoulder is named for the injury many maltsters suffer, caused by turning over huge shovels of sprouting grain on malting house floors. Monkey Shoulder is a big whisky in mouthfeel and flavor. Golden in color, the whisky features a citrus aroma, with notes of cinnamon, clove, and honeysuckle, and whiffs of smoke. A lovely whisky that stands up well to ice and stands out in a cocktail. It's great with ginger ale or soda water and makes a sophisticated Old Fashioned and a terrific Whisky Smash.

Compass Box Whiskymakers

Compass Box Whiskymakers is not located in Scotland, but this London-based bottler only blends Scottish whiskies. And in doing so, they have become one of the premier bottlers in the business. They have a reputation for breaking rules in almost every direction, and are releasing some of the most exciting blends the industry has seen in years.

OK, so, what is a Whiskymaker? The folks at Compass Box invented the term, writing on their company webpage, "To us, a Whiskymaker is someone who feels a need and an obligation to make things better—to ask questions, to challenge, to experiment."

Compass Box does not distill whiskies but rather buys malt whiskies and grain whiskies from designated partners. For malts, they tend to work with Ardmore, Caol Ila, Clynelish, Dailuaine, Glen Elgin, Laphroaig, and Teaninich. When acquiring grain whiskies, they work with Cameronbridge and Cambus. They then make their own blends, and age those stocks in a warehouse in Scotland.

Compass Box offers two blended Scotch whiskies. Great King Street is the brand name of their more affordable line, and its "Artist's Blend" is a light, fruity, and spicy blend, while the "Glasgow Blend" is a fuller-bodied whisky with sweet notes of sherry and hints of smoke. Both are great straight, with soda or ginger ale, and in mixed drinks.

The Spice Tree is possibly the most controversial whisky to be released in the last generation. As originally released in 2005, it was a blend of single malts that received a second aging in American oak casks to which French oak inserts (also known as "inner staves") had been added. The Scotch Whisky Association, the Scotch industry watchdog, strongly objected to this process, as they regarded it as being outside the strictures that other Scotch producers were being held to. The SWA insisted that Compass Box discontinue the practice or stop calling the product Scotch. The SWA actually threatened legal action against Compass Box, demanding an immediate halt to production. In response, Glaser invented a new cask for the secondary aging stage, with a body constructed of American oak staves and a toasted French oak head. This is a massive innovation in both barrel and Scotch whisky making! Spice Tree is among my favorite blended malt Scotch whiskies. Vibrant vanilla and orange notes, with the subtleties of brown sugar, caramel, and dried fruit, this is an exceptionally smooth whisky, one to enjoy neat with a little water back or a single cube. Something to savor.

Compass Box Peat Monster is a blended malt version of the big, smoky whiskies usually associated with Islay. Peat Monster is made from what is assumed to be a blend of Clynelish, Ardmore, Laphroaig, Caol Ila, Ledaig, and more. The whisky is matured in 70 percent new American oak and 30 percent second use American oak. The nose starts off with a big dose of vanilla, marmalade, and dried fruit. There's also a lovely note of brine, and a lot of spice and smoke. Perfect to sip in front of a fireplace or a campfire. Enjoy it with salmon and cheese and crusty bread. Salted peanuts. Leather chairs and mahogany-paneled rooms. This is big boy whisky.

Rock Island Blended Malt Whisky

Douglas Laing & Co. is one of the most innovative independent, family-owned bottlers in Scotland. Established in 1948, its offices are located in Glasgow. In the 2010s, Laing released four blended Scotch whiskies that were massive successes, including Big Peat from Islay, Scallywag from Speyside, Timorous Beastie from the Highlands, and Rock Island Blended Malt Scotch Whisky. All were fantastic, but my favorite was Rock Oyster, which includes malt whiskies from the islands of Jura, Islay, Arran, and Orkney. The whisky has a sweetness to it, but also tastes of the ocean, and is a big homage to the Islands region of Scotland. With lovely honey, caramel, and citrus zest, there's also a salinity (a reminder of the sea) as well as a hint of seaweed and a nice touch of smoke. But the lingering flavor returns to a slight sweetness. Close your eyes and you are on the rocky shores of the Scottish islands. A very special blend. This is an exceptional example of what the art of blending is all about.

A FEW OTHERS TO CONSIDER

Chivas Regal is one of my old-timey favorites. It's made from a blend of single malt and grain whiskies, including malts from Strathclyde and Longmorn distilleries, as well as the famed Strathisla distillery.

Highly coveted is That Boutique-y Whisky Company's Blended Scotch Whiskey #1, one of the most sought-after and hard-to-find whisky blends there is. There is no light whisky base in this blend. Instead, it is a mixture of single malt Scotch whiskies from different houses and therefore cannot be called single malt—but it can be called a blended single malt. It is a little bigger and chewier than traditional blended Scotch whiskies.

Sheep Dip is constructed from sixteen different single malt whiskies from the Lowland, Highland, Speyside, and Islay whisky regions of Scotland. The whisky is dark, old, and has a big nose, highlighting marmalade and dried fruits such as apple, pear, and apricot, with hints of wood, cinnamon, brown sugar, butterscotch, and smoke. Great long finish. A great smoky Scotch.

Blended Whiskey in America

In America, craft distillers brought back blended whiskey in a big way when the whiskey boom first hit, though the trend has waned (bourbon and rye now dominate). Classic American blended whiskey labels include Philadelphia Blended Whiskey, Fleischmann's Preferred Blended Whiskey, and Heaven Hill Kentucky Blended Whiskey, among many. Several craft brands worth searching out include Joshua Tree Distilling Lost Horse Whiskey, Eastside Distilling Barrel Hitch American Blend Whiskey, and Firestone & Robertson Distilling Co.'s TX Blended Whiskey.

One of my favorite quality producers is FEW Spirits. Paul Hletko founded the distillery in 2011, in Evanston, Illinois, once a hotbed of Prohibition bootlegging. Rather than just blending some indiscriminate whiskies, Hletko (who is also the master distiller) decided to take the category in a completely different direction. FEW Spirits American Whiskey is a blend of FEW's bourbon, rye, and malt whiskey (which is cherrywood smoked). This is a lovely sipping whiskey. Soft, approachable. It leads off with honey and toffee, then shortbread, caramel, and a hint of lovely Christmas spice, as well as a faint hint of smoke. It is a well-rounded, exceptional blended whiskey. A great beginner whiskey.

SINGLE MALT SCOTCH WHISKY

There once was a man named Michael Jackson. Not he of one-gloved fame—*the* Michael Jackson, in the UK and around the world, who was the ambassador of fine beer and whisky starting in the late 1970s. It was men like him and Garrett Oliver who made the persuasive argument that beer and whisky deserved to be appreciated like fine wine. That beer required different glasses (not just pint glasses), and that both paired well with exceptional international cuisine.

Michael Jackson was a complicated man. And a talented one. I first met him when I was the associate publisher at Running Press, and we published several of his books. He had long been involved in the publishing industry; it is little known that he was one of the original founding partners of Quarto, one of the world's largest illustrated book publishers at that time. Michael published *The World Guide to Beer* in 1977, and it went on to live a good twenty years in various editions. *Michael Jackson's Malt Whisky Companion* was published in the 1990s. His books sold more than three million copies worldwide.

Michael was already a popular figure in the beer and single malt Scotch world when I met him. He was a television star, with his hit British television show *The Beer Hunter*, which ran in the late 1980s and early 1990s. The beer world adored him. And he was already considered the grand wizard of the single malt Scotch universe. He was a disheveled looking chap, always in gray trousers, a rumpled corduroy jacket, and hair that looked like a wilting afro, like an English professor who'd failed the audition for Grand Funk Railroad.

Michael was quiet, unassuming, and slightly suspicious of people. He was always peering over his glasses at you. He was not entirely chatty. Yet, get him in front of a crowd, and he was fantastic. Regardless of whether it was a beer or whisky crowd, he was an amazing person to watch and listen to. His understanding of the two elixirs was unmatched.

He had a terrific memory, and could relate vast sums of knowledge about brewers around the world and distillers in Scotland. He could explain the flavors you were tasting, how they had been achieved, what the components were, who the distiller or brewer was, and the name of their underlings.

Michael traveled extensively, and I heard from him (or someone in his office, or his agent) at least two or three times a year. He would come to the U.S. from the U.K. for a series of tour dates. I always knew when he was in town because we would get an irate call, asking why there weren't enough books in the stores. Of course, he never told us when he was going to be in the country. This was back in the days before social media, when everything was communicated by fax or phone. We would argue. I would plead with him to let us know in advance when he was coming, so that we might load the markets where he would appear. He'd come in for lunch, or into town for a tasting, and by the next day he would leave. And we were all friends again. Of course, even after he agreed to keep us abreast of his next tour, he absolutely never did.

The first single malt tasting I ever went to was with Michael Jackson. As we entered the large banquet room, he was mobbed and glad-handed by at least a hundred admirers. He shook hands, peered over his glasses, and nodded his head a lot. But once all the hoopla died down, he began in earnest, and I was amazed at how complicated it all was, and how he attempted to simplify it. He was a proselytizer and a prophet all in one, one who foretold the greatness of single malt scotch. I will never forget that first experience. The single malt Scotch world and, by extension, the single malt whisky world owes Michael a huge debt of gratitude.

Michael spent a lifetime educating the public on beer and single malt. His influence on each industry, especially single malt Scotch, was powerful and undeniable. And his presence in a room was mesmerizing to those who wanted to learn. He was never loud. People quieted down to listen to him. He educated thousands of people over the course of his career personally and millions more via his written word and TV show.

Michael died of a heart attack in 2007. So great was his stature that Glenfiddich saluted him with a new release of its Glenfiddich Rare Collection 40 Year Old Single Malt Scotch Whisky in 2008. Many have attempted to fill the vacuum Michael left but there is no one who ever can. Single malt whisky today enjoys a new explosion, a new birth, the world over. It would have been interesting to see Michael's reaction to it, peering over the rim of those glasses. Regardless, he would have complained there were not enough books in the stores.

SINGLE MALT SCOTCH WHISKY 101

According to experts at Johnnie Walker, "The earliest whisky was fairly bracing stuff, distilled almost exclusively by monks. It was never allowed to mature and tended to be very raw, as befitted a drink that was seen primarily as a medicine." However, times changed.

George Smith, a farmer in the Livet valley, founded what essentially became the Glenlivet Distillery in 1824. It was the first licensed distillery in Scotland. He made single malt Scotch. Other whisky makers followed Smith, and by 1830 there were more than 230 licensed distilleries in Scotland. Many of them used traditional pot stills, which produced intense flavors but were inefficient.

Also in 1830, Aeneas Coffey patented his sectional still, known as the Coffey still, a precursor to today's column still. Coffey's innovation was much more efficient and economical than the traditional pot still, as it allowed for continuous distillation, dramatically increasing production.

And when the distillers used a variety of grains, it produced a lighter whisky.

Clever merchants began blending the malt whisky they obtained with grain whisky. These were among the first blended Scotch whiskies, and they became all the rage. By the 1850s, single malt whisky had become a niche market aimed at whisky connoisseurs. Blended Scotch took off like a rocket, and it's what most of the world drank until the early 1960s.

Yes, that's right. For a long time few people, and mostly locals, drank single malt whisky. None were bottled for popular consumption until 1963. (After the single malt craze began, certain distilleries and bottlers packaged older vintages, but it was rare before 1963.)

In broad strokes, what differentiates single malt from other whiskies? Single malt is made from 100 percent malted barley. It must be distilled at a single distillery, using pot still distillation. It must be aged in once-used bourbon barrels. It must not be blended with any whisky from any other distillery. And, of course, Scotch can only come from Scotland.

NOTABLE EXPRESSIONS – HIGHLAND SINGLE MALTS

I love Highland single malt whisky. It is, perhaps, one of my favorite whisky categories. And the variety within the group is so subtle, and yet substantial. Some are completely austere, dry, and bold. Others have fruit and nose, and lingering sweetness that astonishes, without being cloying in any way. Others exhibit characteristics more closely associated with great cognacs. To me, Highland single malts are the best whiskies. They are the Bordeaux red wine of the whisky world. Not that there aren't other good whiskies being made around the world. But after I experiment with a new region, a new style, a new grain, a new process, slowly, without trying to, I always return to the Highlands.

Glenfiddich

In the summer of 1886, William Grant, along with his seven sons and two daughters, began building a distillery by hand. He named it Glenfiddich, Gaelic for Valley of the Deer. The following year, the first drops of spirit came out of their copper stills.

By 1957, Charles Gordon, William's great-grandson, was running the distillery, and insisted on having a coppersmith onsite. Two years later, Gordon Grant built an onsite cooperage, which exists to this day.

In 1961 Glenfiddich further refined its iconic presence with a redesign of its bottle by influential designer Hans Schleger, who created their now renowned and signature triangular bottle. Two years later, Glenfiddich was the first single malt whisky to be actively promoted outside of Scotland. In the U.S., American connoisseurs embraced the "new" whisky, especially those who had been stationed in the U.K. during the war. But it was still a limited market. Even by 1970, according to the *New York Times*, less than 1 in 10 whisky drinkers had ever tried a single malt whisky.

In 1971, the distillery was completely re-outfitted. By 1977, Glenlivet, Glenfiddich, Lagavulin, and Cardhu had joined the chase for the single malt whisky market. But by 1980, vodka, gin, rum, and tequila had transformed the liquor market, and all whiskies struggled. But the Glenfiddich brand and the category continued to climb despite the cocktail trends. Scotland's Whisky Trail was established in the early 1980s, and was a massive hit; Glenfiddich's visitor center was entertaining as many as 50,000 people a year.

In 1987 Glenfiddich celebrated its 100-year anniversary with a centenary bottling commemorating the founder. In 2001 they released their oldest single malt whisky, cask 843, which was filled in 1937. Only sixty-one bottles of this very rare whisky were bottled.

Today Glenfiddich, still entirely family owned, is the top-selling single malt Scotch whisky, followed by Glenlivet, Macallan, Singleton, Glenmorangie, Balvenie, Laphroaig, and a host of others. But the Glenfiddich 12 Year Old is the epitome of single malt Scotch. When you're drinking Glenfiddich, you're drinking history.

"Take the entry-level 12 year old, the foundation for the distillery's No. 1 sales position. It's nearly impossible to find a better single malt for the price, with only The Glenlivet 12 Year Old rivaling it as the quintessential bang for your buck premium Scotch whisky," wrote Richard Thomas, world-renowned whisky authority. "The reason people around the world drink it in such quantity isn't because they are ignorant and tasteless, but because it offers such good value."

This golden-colored whisky starts with notes of fresh pear and apple on the nose, with hints of honey or brown sugar and biscuit. There's a slight sweetness on the palate, as the pear follows through. Hints of butterscotch, cream, and toasty oak. A long, smooth, mellow finish follows. Cream and butterscotch linger.

I tend to like my single malt Scotch neat, with water and ice back. I'll sip it first, and then it depends upon the mood and the weather. In the winter, maybe one rock? In the summer, maybe on the rocks. Some people feel like it makes a great highball with soda water or ginger ale. A lovely, easy drinking whisky.

The Balvenie

William Grant, of Glenfiddich, was born on December 19, 1839. He became a bookkeeper at Mortlach distillery in 1866. He later purchased property near Balvenie Castle, and founded William Grant & Sons distillery in 1887. They began by converting the Balvenie House in early 1892 into a distillery. The Balvenie name would later become the label of the distillery's highest expression of whisky.

David Stewart MBE began his career with William Grant & Sons in 1962. He has now served the company for over sixty years as its malt master. Stewart invented the process that is now known as wood finishing, and created the first blends to be finished in second reuse casks (with the goal of adding more complexity, depth, and flavor) in 1982 when he introduced Grant's Ale Cask Reserve and Grant's Sherry Cask Reserve. Stewart's biggest success was the release of The Balvenie DoubleWood 12 in 1993. While some curmudgeons treated his innovation as a gimmick, it soon became a hallmark of the industry.

When Stewart took over the distillery in the 1980s, within William Grant & Sons the Balvenie label was cast as a boutique production, representing the corporation's high-end product. Their distillery is one of only seven distilleries of more than 120 in Scotland that floor malts its own barley. It is also the only one to grow its own barley and malt its own barley, as well as having an onsite coppersmith and cooperage.

If ever there was a first taste where I fell in love with single malt Scotch, it was DoubleWood 12. The current edition of the whisky is first aged in

American oak ex-bourbon barrels and hogsheads. After twelve years, it is rebarreled in Spanish oak ex-oloroso sherry casks for an additional nine months. On the nose there are figs and dates (provided by the oloroso barrels), along with cherries and dark chocolate, with notes of honey and vanilla. A nutty sweetness first strikes across the palate, with the figs, dates, and ripe pear, followed by Christmas spices, dark brown sugar, and a hint of sweet old brown sherry. It has a lovely, long, warming finish with lingering notes of dark brown sugar and dates and figs. Never sweet. Just an absolutely outstanding, well-balanced, and complex whisky. Never, ever, put this in a cocktail. Water and ice back is all you need—if that. The Caribbean Cask finish is also excellent.

Aberfeldy, Glenfarclas & Glenmorangie

I love many other single malts from Scotland but I absolutely love Aberfeldy 12 Year Old and Glenfarclas 10 Year Old. Both are exceptional whiskies and tremendous values. I also truly love Glenmorangie's 10 Year Old, Quinta Ruban 14 Year Old, and Malaga Cask Finish.

The Aberfeldy 12 Year Old is smooth and sweet, with notes of apple and pear, toffee, biscuit, apricot, and honey with vanilla. An absolutely wonderful sipper.

The Glenfarclas 10 Year Old is a super easy-drinking bottle. Notes of dried fruit, hints of shortbread and brown sugar, as well as spice. A lovely, golden, long-lasting finish, where vanilla lingers. The kind of whisky you'll absolutely enjoy!

The Glenmorangie 10 Year Old is one of the classics of the Scotch world. The whisky, aged in ex-Jack Daniel's and ex-Heaven Hill bourbon barrels, has cognac-like flavors of orange zest, honey, and vanilla, with notes of apple and pear, along with caramel and toffee. The Quinta Ruban 14 Year Old is aged for fourteen years in ex-bourbon barrels and then in port casks from Portugal. The same classic Glenmorangie, but with sweet notes of dates and figs, cocoa, dark caramel, and walnuts. Incredible mouthfeel, with a long, silky finish. The Malaga Cask 12 Year Old is aged in ex-Malaga casks; Malaga wines from the south of Spain are sweet and rich, and referred to as "Malaga dulce." Those same sweet flavors blend with the whisky, adding notes of raisins, dates, honey, and brown sugar. You can't go wrong with Glenmorangie.

NOTABLE EXPRESSIONS – PEATED SINGLE MALTS

For those who like a smokier dram, there is the other style of Scotch whisky—Islay and the other peated whiskies from Speyside and the Islands, for example. These are made by a process that includes smoking the malted barley in a kiln with dried peat. The resulting flavor carries through to the distillate that comes out the still. Peat has been used to warm homes for more than a millennia. Harvested from bogs, it is a local resource in Islay and the other Island regions, and it produces a distinctive aroma when burned.

If there is one man who I think of when I think of smoky Scotch, it is my friend, publisher and photographer, John Whalen. John and I have known each other more than twenty years, and we have traveled far and wide together. No matter where we have gone, whether it be New England, Canada, the Mid-Atlantic, and beyond, at a bar or in a restaurant, John's eyes scan the menu or the backbar looking for his smoky favorites. A bar only gets his approval when he finds one or two of them.

John loves the two most famous peated Scotch producers in the world—Laphroaig and Lagavulin. When his glass arrives, he takes a big whiff, inhaling the campfire-scented elixir. A smile comes across his face. I once asked him how he, an Irishman by descent, had gotten into the peated world of Scotch. He told me, "My brother-in-law said, you're not serious about whisky unless you're drinking Scotch." That brother-in-law liked Islay whisky. "I ventured into Macallan for a while, but then discovered Islay whiskies and I never went back. I started off with Cardhu (one of the single malts in Johnnie Walker Black). It wasn't as smoky as Islay Scotch, but fantastic just the same," said John. "Cardhu was my go-to for years. But now I love Laphroaig, that's truly my favorite Scotch for daily drinking. Lagavulin is for special occasions." John also loves Bunnahabhain and Ardbeg. The Three Distilleries Path, just off Port Ellen's High Street, a three-mile walking path, connects all three distilleries—Laphroaig, Lagavulin, and Ardbeg. It makes for a long but great day of tasting. An aficionado, John has been to all three.

"When I pour a dram of Ardbeg, my family leaves the room, it's so 'aromatic.' It's totally against their idea of an enjoyable aroma!" But John loves it.

Like most devout peated whisky lovers, John prefers his whisky neat. But "over a big rock thereafter for a night of long-distance drinking." John's and my long-distance drinking may be behind us. Not like back in the day, when the two of us got pulled into the CFO's office for a good chewing out over a very expensive tab for two in Toronto. But we still share a dram or two when possible.

When you think of Islay, you're in the Inner Hebrides; this is where they make Harris tweeds. These are cold, misty shores, facing the ocean, which lends a salinity to these whiskies as well. They are as rugged as the shores they were made on.

Laphroaig

Laphroaig Distillery is the first distillery on the Three Distilleries Path. It is at the head of Loch Laphroaig on the south coast of the Isle of Islay. They have been distilling for more than 200 years, founded in 1815 by Donald and Alexander Johnston.

Laphroaig has several features that are distinctive to its works. First is the iconic "pagoda" styled kiln chimney. Another is their malting floor; it is one of the few distilleries in Scotland to still do this in-house. Laphroaig is known for its big, peaty, smoky presence, and has a dedicated fan base, highly prized by whisky experts.

Laphroaig offers a number of different releases. The Laphroaig 10 Year Old is their flagship whisky. The 16 Year Old (another specialty bottling) is also nice, as well as a wide range of other finishes, but the Triple Wood is among my favorites. John's too! It is aged in three different types of casks. Then, after a time, select barrels, ranging in age, are blended and transferred into nineteenth-century quarter casks for a second maturation. Lastly, the whisky is finished in large European oak ex-oloroso sherry casks. Triple Wood is softer than some of Laphroaig's other releases, with a hint more sweetness to juxtapose against the smoke. The nose features raisins and apricots and campfire. Sweet dried fruits like apple, pear, apricot, date, and fig come across the palate, with notes of sherry and toffee. Caramel and vanilla notes linger with the smoke. A beautiful peated whisky.

Lagavulin

Not too far from Lagavulin Bay, on the Isle of Islay, is Lagavulin Distillery, one of the oldest distilleries in Scotland. John Johnston founded the first legal distillery in Scotland on the site in 1816. Less than a year later, Archibald Campbell Brooks opened a second distillery. Alexander Graham acquired both, and eventually united them under the name Lagavulin.

Lagavulin is one of the most sought-after single malts in all of Scotland due to the intense smokiness of their whiskies. The malted barley for their single malt has up to twenty times more exposure to peat smoke than other single malt Scotches. Fans of their whisky are almost cultish.

Lagavulin offers many ages and types. The 10 Year Old (a travel retail exclusive at many duty-free shops) and the 16 Year Old are the most popular. The 16 Year Old is a special whisky and one of the most iconic of Islay. It starts with the powerful flavors of a rich sweetness coupled with a light brininess, but is incredibly well balanced with notes of dates, figs, and dark cherries and deep, luscious smoke. Elegant. Stately. Immense complexity, and a long, long finish. An outstanding dram. If you can ever get your hands on the Lagavulin Distillers Edition, by all means do it! It is a robust whisky, with a hint more oak. As John says, a holiday treat!

Ardbeg

Last but certainly not least along the Three Distilleries Path is Ardbeg Distillery. Ardbeg began distilling in 1798, and by 1887 the distillery produced more than 250,000 gallons of whisky per year for inclusion in other whisky brands. The distillery was shuttered in the 1980s, but full production resumed in 1997.

Ardbeg has won several major awards for best whisky in the world since then. The quality definitely measures up against its neighbors. However, Ardbeg has always had an adventurous spirit, and is more akin to a craft spirits producer. They have a number of fanciful offerings, such as Galileo (in 2011, twenty vials of Ardbeg spirit and wood particles were sent to the International Space Station and returned in September of 2014); Fermutation, which featured a three-week fermentation (the distillery's longest such experiment); and BizarreBBQ (inspired by BBQ and whisky).

Their core offerings include Ardbeg Ten Year Old, Ardbeg Wee Beastie, Ardbeg An Oa, Ardbeg Uigeadail, and Ardbeg Corryvreckan. The 10 Year Old is excellent. I love the An Oa and Corryvreckan. An Oa is made from a blend of whiskies aged in different casks, including ex-Pedro Ximenez, charred virgin oak, and ex-bourbon, among others. This is a lovely dram, filled with dark chocolate and dark fruit, with a delicate sweetness that balances beautifully against the smoke. This shows the kind of classic Islay Scotch that Ardbeg is capable of distilling.

Corryveckan is a no-age-statement single malt named for a famous whirlpool to the north of Islay. As Ardbeg says of this release, "Not for the faint hearted." This was named World's Best Single Malt in 2010 by the World Whisky Awards. This is big boy stuff, for the true believers. This particular expression was aged in a mix of American and French oak barrels, and bottled at an impressive 57.1% ABV. In the glass, Corryvreckan is a light golden color, with thick, viscous legs. This is an aromatic dram—you can smell it from a yard away. A huge dose of smoke spirals out of the glass with notes of pine needles and medicinal herbs, but it is balanced by notes of butter and caramel. On the palate there are dark fruits—blueberries, black currants, dark cherries—as well as brine and seaweed, along with clove and caramel. It is a big, chewy, brusque, in-your-face whisky that makes no apologies. Ardbeg is right. It's not for the weak of heart.

SINGLE MALT OUTSIDE OF SCOTLAND

Like many whiskey drinkers, for a long time I was blithely unaware of what was going on in the world of single malt outside of Scotland. But globally a new wave of small craft distillers was slowly emerging. By 2016 there were more than twenty-five countries producing single malts of all kinds.

I remember a story Clay Risen wrote for the *New York Times* in 2013, when I was working with him on his book *American Whiskey, Bourbon & Rye*. "The humid streets of Waco, Tex., may not have much in common with the misty glens of Scotland, home to some of the world's best malt whiskies," wrote Clay. "Not much, that is, until last month, when a single-malt whiskey from the Balcones Distillery in Waco bested nine others, including storied Scottish names like the Balvenie and the Macallan, in a blind panel of British spirits experts. It was the first time an American whiskey won the Best in Glass, a five-year-old competition to find the best whiskey released in a given year."

An American distillery had produced a whiskey that was as good as Scotch? What? Heresy! Behind that bottle was a group of young men as far away from Scotland as one could imagine. And I later got to interview the leader of that group, the incredible Chip Tate.

"One of my proudest moments happened in 2012. I received a call from Neil Ridley in London. He and several other whisky writers and critics had organized a clandestine competition they called Best in Glass," recalled Tate. "In brief, these UK whisky judges organized a whisky competition on their own UK turf focusing around single malt whisky, a traditionally UK product, and picked my American single malt as their favorite. I was shocked. Part of the shock could be attributed to the fact I did not even know my malt was in the competition, no doubt. But even more shocking was that UK whisky critics had organized a UK whisky competition and chosen an American single malt as their favorite."

Of course, I finally tasted the Balcones. It was amazing. Big, bold, sweet, chewy. Balcones "1" Texas Single Malt Classic Edition is 100 percent malted grain, distilled in hammered copper pot stills, aged in new American oak barrels, and non-chill filtered. The nose leads with butter, baked pears and apples, honey, toffee, and tropical fruits. It is smooth and silky on the palate, a big bowl of dates and figs along with marmalade and more butter, and finishes with buttered toffee and notes of oak. A fantastic dram.

Eventually, Tate began to see that the victory was a triumph that extended well beyond him.

"I began to understand that the most important victory was not a personal one, as gratifying as it was. I realized in that moment that new things were possible for malt whisky around the world," said Tate. "This quiet malt whisky revolution has been going on for decades. But only now are the malts of these labors becoming more known to the broader whisky world."

Balcones won in January 2013. The Japanese won a different competition later that year. I, like many others, bull-rushed the liquor stores, scouring the shelves, looking for these new Japanese unicorns—alas, they were hard to find. But the surprises in those bottles were extraordinary once you were able to obtain a sip—maybe a dram from a very good whiskey menu or bar. The Japanese whiskies were so light, and floral, and had a sweetness. By contrast, whiskies like Balcones, Del Bac, Sons of Liberty, and Notch were robust and oh so very American in their richness and their big oak. Kavalan from Taiwan was an eye opener. Starward from Australia blew me away.

Friends who were devoted Scotch fans and dyed-in-the-wool (especially Harris Tweed) types scoffed. "That's not real single malt!" The hell it wasn't. Many of these distilleries were following much of the guidelines established by the Scotch Whisky Association but adapted for home use. Americans used American oak. In some cases they even used their state's oak. The Japanese used mizunara oak instead of American or in addition to American. But many stuck to the same principles. One hundred percent barley. Aged. Unblended. Made and aged and bottled by the same company.

Other similar successes soon followed. Triple Eight Distillery's Notch, an upstart from Nantucket Island in Massachusetts, was surprisingly awarded the Trophy for Best American Single Malt 11 Years and Older by the International Spirit Challenge in 2016. Other upsets followed. By 2018, when Jim Murray, currently the most famous arbiter of whisky quality in the world, named his top five single malts from around the globe for that year's *Whisky Bible*, none of them were from Scotland. It was the first time in eighteen editions that not a single Scotch made his list. The single malt world had been turned upside down.

"The real story today isn't the growth of sales, but the growth of the category—it's not your grandfather's single malt. Yes, the Glens are still going strong. But so is Bastille in France and Nikka in Japan," wrote Risen in his *New York Times* article. "The United States has a robust single malt scene along the West Coast (which isn't to slight the great single malts coming out of New England and Texas and various points in between). Name a country, and these days there's probably a single malt distillery somewhere. And not just the obvious, temperate, and culturally British places like Australia and South Africa, but places like Taiwan and Italy as well."

The mainstream press could not cover the boom adequately or fast enough. Many had been asleep at the wheel. Others were overwhelmed by the explosion. Soon networks of writers, journalists, and bloggers were exchanging notes and writing reviews, making recommendations all across the internet as the category blew up. The world could not keep up.

I largely managed to, but barely.

One of my favorite memories from that time was chasing down the bottles from New England and New York distilleries. I made pilgrimages all over the Northeast. I coveted and acquired bottles of single malt whiskies much like Gollum (Smeagol) fetishized the Ring he called "precious." I collected Hillrock Estate and Tuthilltown in the Hudson Valley, Nashoba's Stimulus, Boston Harbor Distillery's Putnam Single Malt, and Triple Eight Distillery's The Notch Nantucket Island, from Massachusetts.

One of my most memorable trips was to the Sons of Liberty distillery in Rhode Island. I first tasted Sons of Liberty at a massive whiskey-tasting show in Manhattan before I ever knew anything about them. I didn't know where they were from or who they were. But out of more than a hundred whiskies that day, their products stood out! Done!

Sons of Liberty, in history, was a secret society of citizens in the American Colonies who organized in an attempt to protect the rights of colonists and to oppose unfair taxation. Theirs was the famed motto "No taxation without representation."

Enter Mike Reppucci who thought it would be a good idea to try to make world-class whiskey in New England, so he founded Sons of Liberty Spirits Co. "A little known fact, even among regular whiskey drinkers, is that all whiskey starts as beer," says Mike. "For years, craft brewers have been producing outstanding seasonal brews, and we saw the opportunity to advance the trend to American craft whiskey."

Mike wanted to make a single-malt whiskey. That's when he turned to the famed master distiller Dave Pickerell to begin experimenting with recipes using different beers. They finally settled on a stout that featured 100 percent barley malts like chocolate malt, crystal 45, and biscuit malt, among others. They double distilled the beer after it was finished. They aged the distillate in a combination of charred new American oak and toasted French oak barrels to give it added complexity.

The nose on Sons of Liberty Uprising American Single Malt Whiskey starts with cocoa and coffee, along with apples and figs, vanilla, and caramel. Apple, cocoa, vanilla, caramel, and honey all come through on the palate. There is a hint of spice at the end. The finish, surprisingly, is vanilla and cream and is dry and clean. To me, this whiskey finishes lighter and drier than it smells. Maybe because the roasts suggest it, but I was expecting a bit more brown sugar. But that is me being picky.

This is a wonderful whiskey. Well executed. Beautifully done. As it did to me when I first tasted it, it will open your eyes! Strike another blow for the Sons of Liberty and for Rhode Island! Their other single malt, Battle Cry American Single Malt, is made from a Belgian-style ale with a mash bill of 100 percent malted rye and honey malt. They use a Trappist-style yeast strain to ferment the distiller's beer. The spirit is then aged in charred new American oak barrels. The whiskey has hints of orange marmalade, dark butterscotch, coffee, caramel, and spice. It's got a big, sweet, chewy mouthfeel, and a long, long finish, filled with baked apple and hints of sweetness combined with tang. A fantastic, unique experience.

Both of these whiskies are uniquely American. And they must be tried. I liked them so much that when I came out with my first malt whiskey book, Mike asked me to come up and do a tasting and talk. Forty people attended and we had a great evening. It was so successful, Mike asked us to stay after hours for a few drinks. I tell you, when the night began, after the tasting, I was stone cold sober. But they had this rakish British mixologist who started dealing out cocktails like baseball cards—a Martini, a Boulevardier, a Manhattan, an Old Fashioned. I don't recommend this course of action to anyone. Suffice to say, at three a.m. I woke up in a pitch-black hotel room, in my bed, naked, and covered in chocolate bars. Apparently, I had gone to the vending machine to get a soda but instead came back with my arms full of every chocolate bar in the machine, and promptly passed out. Suffice to say, there is much, much more to the story (more than slightly Hunter S. Thompson-esque). If I see you, and you ask me, I'll fill you in. But don't let this stop you. Get to Mike's distillery and try these two fantastic whiskies.

Other great single malts from the United States include Westward Whiskey (Oregon), Defiant (North Carolina), Whiskey Del Bac (Arizona), Rogue Spirits (Oregon), and Stranahan's (Colorado). Great single malts from Canada include Shelter Point (British Columbia), Eau Claire (Alberta), and Still Waters (Ontario).

India has two shining stars in the single malt arena, Amrut and Paul John. It is perhaps no surprise that India, with long, long ties to Britain, should have such a fondness for single malt. And like the Scotch, they spell whisky with just the "y."

Amrut Single Malt is produced by Amrut Distilleries, and is the first single malt whisky to be made in India. Amrut (अमृत) is Sanskrit and means "nectar of the gods." And so it is. JN Radhakrishna Rao Jagdale founded Amrut Laboratories in Bangalore, Karnataka, in 1947. A year later he founded the distillery, first making brandy. Amrut Single Malt Whisky was launched in Europe in 2004. The whisky is smooth drinking, much in the Speyside style. Made from six-row

Indian barley, and aged in ex-American bourbon casks for about four years, it features notes of graham cracker, cantaloupe, apricot, apple, toffee, and caramel. An easy whisky to like.

Another recent entry from India is Paul John Single Malt Whisky. Manufactured by John Distilleries, the company's first distillery was also set up in Bangalore. The brand launched its first whisky, Paul John Single Cask 161 Whisky, in London in 2012. The company grew quickly. By 2009 it had eight production facilities, and sold more than 12 million cases that year, and an ownership stake and distribution deal with Sazerac.

Paul John produces three core labels and issues an annual Christmas release, as well as several other smaller series. Paul John Brilliance Indian Single Malt is the flagship of the core whiskies. It is made in Goa, and produced using Indian six-row malted barley. They smoke their malted barley with imported Islay and Aberdeen peat. It is distilled in traditional copper pot stills and aged ex-American bourbon barrels. Honey, demerara sugar, and some spice lead the attack, with notes of toffee, figs, raisins, apple, and intense vanilla. Super easy to drink in the best sense.

One of the most remarkable single malts in the world comes from Taiwan, Kavalan Solist Vinho Barrique. Kavalan is the old name of Yilan County, in Taiwan. Distillery construction finished in December 2005. The first spirits were drawn in March 2006. Kavalan launched its first bottling in December 2008. It has three core bottlings: Classic Single Malt Whisky, Triple Sherry Cask, and Solist Vinho Barrique Single Cask Strength. Upon all their releases Kavalan garnered great reviews. The Solist Vinho Barrique is absolutely a massive standout. It's first aged in ex-American bourbon barrels, then finished in a series of former red and white wine casks. Cereal and toasty oak, caramel, vanilla, spice, pepper, and a certain sweetness (from the wine casks) make this cask strength whisky something really unique.

Many wonderful single malts are coming from other parts of Europe. Brenne Whisky and Warenghem, both in France, make some special products. Brenne's founder, Allison Parc, literally began by pedaling her product around New York City on a Citi Bank Bike in 2012.

The first release, Brenne Estate Cask, sold out in two months. Brenne Ten French Single Malt Whisky was introduced three years later, and by that time, the whisky was being distributed in more than thirty-five states. Brenne Ten is made from two different heirloom two-row barleys that are twice distilled in an alembic Charente still, then aged in new French Limousin oak and cognac casks. The whisky is proofed with water from the Charente river. The result is a light to medium–bodied whisky that includes cognac-like features of stone fruit, orange zest, and a certain flintiness. Fruit-forward tropical notes, honey, light brown sugar, and dried fruits are all throughout, finishing with a lovely creaminess. A fantastic whisky.

Warenghem Distillery in Lannion (not far from Brest) dates back to 1900, and has produced some prodigious products in its history. There are three Armorik Whisky Breton single malts: Classic, Double Maturation, and Sherry Cask. All are good, but the Double Maturation and Sherry Cask are my favorites. Double Maturation Whisky first lives in Breton oak barrels, and is finished in ex-oloroso sherry casks. The Sherry Cask is aged directly in ex-sherry casks. I am a sucker for those signature sherry note finishes of dates, figs, and brown sugar. Amazing.

When most people think of Spain, they think of wine. Their wine-growing regions are legendary and with good reason. However, Spain is also known for the diversity and quality of its spirits and liquors, producing some of the best and most unique brandies, rums, and gins in the world. So there was a rich tradition of distilling to draw on when the Destilerías y Crianza del Whisky S.A. (DYC) was originally established in 1958 to make whisky. By 1963, the first Spanish whisky was released, a popular and inexpensive brand produced specifically for the domestic market. Today, DYC is a subsidiary of Beam Suntory, and produces high-quality products for domestic consumption as well as for export. DYC Single Malt Whisky 10 Year Old is a simple, direct whisky with a light touch of sugar, dried fruits, honey, brown sugar, and vanilla. It's an easy drinking dram, a solid introductory single malt, and quite a good cocktail mixer.

In the mid- to late-1990s several groups of Scandinavian whisky and distilling enthusiasts wondered why there weren't more single malt whiskies from their region. That has been rectified in the last two decades, with a steady stream of some of the most impressive single malt whiskies in the world coming out of Scandinavia. And industry insiders can only see more good things happening.

The most famous single malt whiskey brands from Sweden are Mackmyra, Smögen, and Hven. Mackmyra has two mainstays, among others: Mackmyra Svensk Ek and Mackmyra Svensk Rök. The first is aged in Swedish oak, and the second is smoked, using local dried peat and juniper twigs. Both are excellent.

Meanwhile, in Ireland, The Tyrconnell, Teeling, and Glendalough Distillery make some absolutely outrageous single malt whiskies. Teeling Single Malt Irish Whiskey is lovely—brilliant, complex, well balanced, and beautiful to drink. The Tyrconnell and Glendalough are equally interesting. And there are many more coming from Ireland these days.

Smögen is a small craft producer making exceptional products, and Hven is a major gin producer that is also producing numerous wonderful, rich single malt whiskies, including their Seven Stars series. Stauning Danish Whisky produces some super impressive single malts, as does Millstone, which hails from the Netherlands.

Some astonishing whiskies come from the land down under. I know, I know. But the whiskies are surprisingly good. Sullivans Cove Distillery was established in Tasmania in 1994, and has never looked back. They offer a long line of single barrel releases of single malt whiskies that will blow you away. Their Double Cask, the best of their single malts, is amazingly rich and warm, and lingers like crazy.

Starward's Nova Single Malt Australian Whisky, made in Port Melbourne, is one of the country's signature single malts. Double distilled and made with Australian malted barley, it is aged in winery barrels from the Yarra Valley and Barossa Valley. It is light-to-medium bodied with flavors of fresh berries, pears, and apples, as well as notes of caramel and spice. Vanilla and fruit linger on the finish, with a bit of light brown sugar. Stellar.

The good news is, you don't have to drink so much that you find yourself lying in the dark, wondering where the hell you are, and why you are covered in chocolate. You only have to go to a good bar with a great whiskey menu or a retail shop with a good whiskey selection to find some of these amazing whiskies. I promise you, you and your friends will be pleasantly surprised.

"What whisky will not cure, there is no cure for."

—Irish Proverb

IRISH WHISKEY

My earliest memory of Irish whiskey is seeing a bottle of it at Scott Liell's house in New Canaan, Connecticut, in the spring of 1986. I had met Scott in a creative writing course at the University of Connecticut, where I was taking a couple classes to finally finish my college degree.

Upon arriving at Scott's house, I met Scott's equally burly brother, Kurt. These were the kind of guys, especially Kurt, who competed in Connecticut's Scottish Games. Kurt (who reminded me of Hall of Fame football lineman Joe Klecko) competed in the caber toss, where, clad in a kilt, he balanced and then hurled an 18-foot-long, 140-pound log. Big dudes.

I hung out with them and two of their friends. Like many other college-aged kids, we spent countless hours doing stupid things I can't even recall. But I do remember that, in their beautifully appointed house, in the center of the kitchen table, sat a bottle of Jameson Irish Whiskey. It seemed almost spotlighted in my memory. It was their father's whiskey, but that did not stop us from trying it.

Jameson is an Irish blended whiskey. The word "whiskey" comes from the Irish *uisce beatha*, or "water of life." At one point, Irish whiskey was the best-selling spirit in the world.

We each poured a shot's worth, and swallowed hard. Our faces contorted, like poison victims, trying to act brave. All except for Kurt. He was younger than me, but did his shot like a man, I thought. Hardly a reaction. Throwing back those shots was a test of manhood, standing around a kitchen table.

I do remember that the second shot, which I was stupid enough to attempt, was much better. It went down much smoother, and with a lot less burn. I began to discern some flavors. And I remember thinking, that really wasn't so bad. But I still needed a glass of water to wash it down.

That was a fun spring and summer. Eventually, Scott and I shared an apartment, and we remained friends until his untimely and devastating death in 2012, when he was only 40. To this day, every time I walk into a restaurant, scan the shelves at the bar, and see the Jameson label, I think back to that period, conjuring the faces of those young men. When the two crazy Liell brothers wrestled and cursed, and we all laughed, and we all sat there, drinking Jameson's.

IRISH WHISKEY 101

The principal difference between Irish whiskey and Scotch whisky is that Scotch is twice distilled and, generally speaking, Irish whiskey is distilled three times, making it a lighter, smoother spirit. Nearly all Irish whiskey was triple distilled in the late nineteenth century. That is not so anymore. Whiskies that contain triple-distilled spirits include blends like Jameson, Midleton, and Tullamore D.E.W., Redbreast, Powers, Green Spot, Irishman, Writers' Tears, Sexton, Glendalough, and Teeling. While triple distillation does provide a certain amount of smoothness, in the new, more opened world of Irish distilling, there is room for different processes. For example, Waterford Irish Single Malt and Cooley's whiskies (including The Connemara and The Tyrconnell) are double distilled.

Irish distillers generally used giant pot stills to produce their whiskey in the 1800s. But they didn't use this process to perfect a smoother whiskey. "In many cases, a third round of distilling was needed to extract more alcohol from the generally lower-yielding mash of malted and unmalted barley," explained Thijs Klaverstijn in *Distiller* magazine. "A pure pot still whiskey is in essence often quite heavier than an average double distilled malt whisky."

Contrary to popular opinion, there are regulations that must be followed for a bottle to carry the label "Irish whiskey." It must be made in Ireland. It must be barrel aged in a 700-liter wooden cask, such as an oak barrel, for at least three years. The whiskey must be made from grains such as barley, wheat, rye, and corn. Water can comprise as much as 60 percent of a bottle of whiskey. Caramel coloring is allowed, but it may not be added for aroma or flavor. Whiskies made in Ireland may be double or triple distilled. The whiskey cannot exceed 94.8% ABV when barreled, and must be a minimum of 40% ABV when bottled. Only four types of whiskey are approved for use in blends in Ireland: Irish, pot still, malt, and grain whiskey. Only pot still, malt, and grain Irish whiskies can be labeled single malt.

Irish whiskey, through a series of troubles, declined from a high of twenty-eight distilleries at the turn of the nineteenth century to only two in 1966—Old Bushmills and Jameson (then at Bow Street and later at Midleton). Both were owned by the same company, Irish Distillers. Since then, the Irish distilling scene has witnessed a massive comeback. The first new distillery in Ireland was Cooley Distillery, founded in 1987. Ireland now has more than thirty distilleries in operation.

NOTABLE EXPRESSIONS

I truly think that the two classic Irish whiskies, Jameson Irish Whiskey and Bushmills The Original, are the two best starter whiskies on the market. They are excellent entry points for the novice whiskey drinker. And they are old, tried-and-true friends for those who have come to love and appreciate the category. Both are solid, easy drinking, enjoyable drams.

Jameson

Jameson Irish whiskey is one of the easiest drinking whiskies I know of. It is a classic blended whiskey, made from combining grain whiskey and single pot still whiskey. The pot still is a mixture of malted and unmalted or "green" Irish barley. All of the grain is sourced from within a fifty-mile radius around the distillery in Cork. The whiskey is barrel aged a minimum of four years in both ex-sherry and ex-bourbon oak barrels and stored in Jameson's warehouses.

The nose on Jameson Original Irish Whiskey is a combination of floral overtones, with spice and wood. There are also notes of dried fruit, honey, and vanilla. On the palate there's vanilla and sherry, as well as walnuts and baking spices. It has a long, lingering note to it, finishing with vanilla and toffee, but it is not sweet. Great on the rocks, in a Highball, or in any cocktail. A fun, easy drinking whiskey.

My true favorite is the Jameson Caskmates Stout Edition, their classic blended whiskey finished in stout barrels. The first editions were aged in barrels from a local brewery in 2013. The whiskey was an immediate hit. I remember sampling it with Dan Kirkhus, an artisanal baker in the Hudson Valley, and a trusted fellow taster. We were instantly won over. Baked apples and pears lead off the nose, with hints of citrus zest, hazelnut, and cocoa. The palate was special, with touches of mocha and milk chocolate, and a lovely dose of vanilla and spices. The chocolate and a light toffee lingered for a long time. This is a sipping whiskey, great neat or with one rock. A light but chewy whiskey, with wonderful aromas and a terrific lingering. The kind of bottle a few friends can just sit with and tell great stories.

Old Bushmills

Old Bushmills traces its history back to 1608, when King James I granted the area a license to distill whiskey. More than 400 years later, they are still at it. Bushmills creates whole lines of whiskies: their classic blends, including The Original, a line of single malts, and some rare limited editions.

Bushmills The Original is a combination of grain whiskey and malt whiskey. The whiskey has notes of vanilla, caramel, pear, and apple, a hint of citrus, honey, and shortbread. It has a long finish, with vanilla, light brown sugar, and shortbread lingering. It is a lovely whiskey. A wonderful, solid whiskey. Great to drink alone or in a cocktail. Makes a lovely Highball.

While The Original is so incredibly well known, I think it is Bushmills Single Malt 12 Year Old that is the real shining star. Yes, they have older, rarer, and much more expensive bottlings that are remarkable. But as an affordable whiskey, it is hard to find a bottle better than their 12 Year Old single malt. The distillate is triple-distilled malt whiskey. It is then aged nine years in ex-bourbon and ex-sherry casks. After that, it is finished in Marsala wine casks. Apples, pears, and nuts are strong on the nose, with a hint of caramel and butter. There is a bit of caramel and notes of dried apple and pear on the palate, along with dark chocolate, tobacco, and more caramel. Spice and nuts present in the aftertaste, as well as lingering vanilla. The whiskey is an excellent sipper, especially neat, but can certainly stand up to ice. I am not one to waste single malt on cocktails, but many writers seem to like this for a Highball or Old Fashioned. No matter, this is an excellent whiskey, well worth seeking out.

Teeling

I first discovered Teeling whiskey when I was researching single malt whiskies from around the world. I became an instant fan of the whiskey and of Jack Teeling, the founder of this iconic Irish craft distillery, and whose own lineage in Irish distilling stretches back to 1782.

Teeling specializes in small batch production whiskies. They produce a small batch Irish whiskey, a single grain, a single malt, a pot still, and a peated single malt. All are exceptional. Teeling Small Batch Irish Whiskey is made from hand-selected barrels of triple-distilled grain and malt whiskey that are cellared in ex-bourbon barrels. The chosen whiskies are then blended and aged in Central American ex-rum casks for another year. The whiskey is bottled at a relatively high 46% ABV. The result is an amazing Irish whiskey that starts off with notes of dried apple, pear, and apricot, vanilla and spice, and hints of rum. On the palate it has honey and vanilla, nuts, and spice. Wood, dried fruits, toffee, spice, and vanilla linger. A unique take on Irish whiskey, with bigger alcohol, layered and complex, and so very impressive. A versatile, sophisticated whiskey that's classy alone or a good companion to others in a glass—perfect for cocktails where you want the whiskey and the alcohol to stand up to mixers.

I also love Teeling Single Pot Still Irish Whiskey, big and chewy, with lots of flavors and complexity. The 100 percent barley mash bill is half malted and half unmalted grain that is then triple distilled. This is a classic Irish mash bill predating Prohibition, reaching back to the glory days when Irish whiskey was the best-selling whiskey in the world. Afterward, it is aged in a combination of new American oak, ex-bourbon, and ex-sherry barrels. Floral and fruity on the nose, with lots of spice on the palate, light brown sugar, and a creamy finish. A truly unique whiskey.

Redbreast

I can't remember the first time I tried Redbreast, but I can remember it was roughly around 2014 or 2015. Famed world whiskey writer Jim Murray had dubbed Redbreast "Liquid Gold" in his annual *Whisky Bible* and in 2013 it was awarded the Double Gold Medal at the San Francisco World Spirits Competition. Suddenly everyone was clamoring for, or singing the praises of, Redbreast. Everyone wanted me to order a Redbreast at lunch, dinner, at cocktail bars. "Have you tried it yet?" "Tell me you love it!" "My new go-to!" It was enough to almost make me resentful.

But Redbreast is not a new label. W&A Gilbey was founded in London in 1857. By 1861, the company had opened a branch on what is now O'Connell Street in Dublin, and had more than 300,000 gallons of whiskey from Dublin distilleries in stock under bond. It blended these whiskies and sold them to consumers under its own labels. The Redbreast label first appeared in 1912. According to legend, Redbreast arrived at its name when the company's then chairman (an avid birdwatcher) decided to name it for the red-breasted robin. The brand suffered ups and downs but remained in use. Gilbey's ceased production of Redbreast in 1985. Irish Distillers bought the brand, and relaunched it in 1991. Originally released as a 12-year-old bottling, Redbreast has gone on to release as 15-year-old, 21-year-old, and other bottlings.

Redbreast Single Pot Still Irish Whiskey 12 Year Old is the flagship of the brand. It has the classic Irish mash bill of half malted and half unmalted barley, triple distilled in copper pot stills. It is then aged in a combination of ex-bourbon barrels and ex-oloroso sherry casks. The nose features apples, apricots, and dates and a hint of toasted oak. Spice, dried fruits, and toffee come across on the palate, as well as a bit of the sherry. Lovely complexity and balance finish, as the dried fruit, toffee, and spices combine nicely. Light and lovely, this whiskey is a great sipper, and a perfect cocktail companion for a Highball or Whiskey Sour.

Spot Whiskey

I first saw and tried Green Spot whiskey at a bar. I took a flier on it, knowing nothing about it; I remember liking it very much but soon forgot about it. Then famed *Malt Advocate* editor and whiskey writer Lew Bryson began speaking and writing about how the Spot whiskies were showing up and which colors to try. Lew is one of the most likeable people in the whiskey and beer worlds. Incredibly knowledgeable, he is always willing to share thoughts and opinions, but never in a nasty way. He has been a mentor and someone to emulate as far as what a spirits writer should be. He is an educator, in the best sense, like Michael Jackson was before him. I began looking for Spot whiskies in earnest. If Lew says it's good, you better run and buy it right away. He once said of tasting the Green, Yellow, and Red Spot whiskies, "It's an enlightening experience doing all three of them."

The flagship is Green Spot Single Pot Still Irish Whiskey, the only bottling that has continued through the company's history. It is very affordable and very well made. A non-age-statement whiskey, the spirits that go into it are aged between seven and ten years in a combination of charred new American oak and ex-bourbon barrels and sherry casks. Bright fruit of apples, pears, and even a hint of peaches combine with cereal and toasted wood to impress the nose. Granny Smith apples and spices come across the palate, with notes of light brown sugar and toasted oak. Sweet barley and baking spices linger on the palate for a nice long time. A light, fresh, fruity, and well-constructed dram.

Red Spot 15 Year Old is also wonderful. It leads off with dried apple and apricot, maybe even golden raisins, and sweet barley, as well as some of the fruit coming from the wine barrels. The wood contributes a lovely backbone to the whiskey without overpowering it. This is a much livelier dram than one might expect of a 15-year-old whiskey. The fruits are still present, if just a touch muted. There is a hint of really good fruitcake. And, of course, there is a hint more oak as well, making it slightly more austere, but in the best possible way.

There are now numerous bottles of Irish whiskey on my shelves and in storage cabinets in my home. There is nothing like sharing a glass of Irish whiskey. It says, "Welcome!" any time you open a bottle. There is an old Irish proverb that says, "What whiskey will not cure, there is no cure for." It's kind of true.

JAPANESE WHISKY

My first memory of Japanese whisky dates back to when I was living in a studio apartment in Times Square in New York in 1986. Back then, the billboards on the north tower of the square dominated the tableaux. During the 1950s and 1960s the names Canadian Club and Admiral Television Appliances glowed there. In 1975 Coca-Cola took Admiral's place. By the end of the 1980s, Suntory's name rose above the crossroads of New York City. And it remained there until the turn of the last century. That was my introduction to the fact that Japan made whisky.

The Japanese have been making whisky for more than a hundred years. Their love of whisky dates back even further, according to Japanese whisky expert Stefan Van Eycken, to Commodore Matthew C. Perry's opening of Japan to the West. Perry sailed to the entrance to Edo Bay in Japan on July 8, 1853. Japan had been closed to the outside world for more than 220 years. Along with a letter from President Millard Fillmore, Perry showered the emperor and the delegation of Japanese officials with many presents, which included American whiskey. A year later, to cement relations with Japan, Perry brought even more whiskey. With the end of seclusion, and a new ruling class, Japan first attempted their own whiskies in the 1870s and 1880s.

Suntory was founded in 1899 by Shinjirō Torii. He opened his first store, Torii Shōten, that year, in Osaka. There he sold all manner of imported wines, and in 1907 expanded to selling port wine. The next expansion was more daring. In 1923, Torii built the Yamazaki Distillery, Japan's first and now oldest malt distillery. Today, it is considered the birthplace of Japanese whisky. But all I knew back then was that Sammy Davis Jr. and Peter Lawford, both of Rat Pack fame, had long been

Suntory spokesmen. I recall Suntory's stunning ads with elaborately painted Japanese theater figures, which were very popular at the time.

Single malt whisky was not bottled and sold until 1964, when Glenfiddich was the first to sell it in their iconic triangular bottles; Japanese distillers took note. In 1976, a very small distillery, Sanraku Ocean, released Karuizawa Single Malt Whisky. In 1984 Keizo Saji, the second son of Suntory founder Torii, insisted the company release a Japanese single malt. Nikka also released their first single malt in 1984, when they offered Hokkaido Single Malt 12 Year Old. Five years later, Nikka released a second single malt, Yoichi 12 Year Old.

I knew none of this until around 2013 when Japanese whiskies seemed to be on the rise. Suntory's 2013 Yamazaki Sherry Cask won "World Whisky of the Year" in 2015 in Jim Murray's *Whisky Bible*. Japanese single malts and blended whiskies took America by storm. "After decades as an also-ran in the American whiskey market, Japanese whiskey is on the ascent," wrote Clay Risen in the *New York Times*. "Suntory's sales in the United States rose 44 percent, according to the company, which found it difficult to keep up with demand. So it increased prices of the Yamazaki 12- and 18-year-olds by 10 percent last year and this year."

It was around this time I bought my first bottle of Hibiki. Then, it was blended from more than twenty different whiskies. It had a lovely nose and a hint of perfume-y sweetness that reportedly came from mizunara oak, the Japanese oak used to make barrels to age Japanese whisky. I had gone to visit my friend Rich up in Lowell, Massachusetts. He had never had Hibiki, so we tasted it together. It was an eye-opener. Rich loved it too. But that's when I got a bigger shock. Living up there in the "middle of nowhere," as I liked to tease, Rich was already an aficionado of Japanese whisky. An intense lover of all Asian cuisines, Rich was not new to Japanese whisky. Who knew?! I did not.

Thus began my "Lost (Japanese whisky) Weekend." He first took me to his favorite sushi restaurant, where we were joined by John Crabtree. Rich and John make up the balance of what I jokingly call our New England Craft Beverage Research Team. Once assembled, we enjoyed a martini and some sushi. Then we sampled a few of the Japanese whiskies there. I was surprised. I thought many of them were light but still immensely flavorful.

Then we went to a ramen bar. The food was amazing. We had steamed baos, an order of pork belly, and another of duck. Then we each had a bowl of ramen, big, hearty portions of broth and vegetables, layered with eggs and meat, and piled high with noodles. It was the perfect counterbalance to the cold New England winter night outside. We tasted several Japanese beers, including Sapporo, Echigo, and Orion. Afterward, we talked whisky with co-owner Peter Huynh, a Japanese whisky enthusiast. He proudly explained what he knew about Japanese whisky and poured us many drams. We started off with Mars Whisky's Iwai, Suntory Whisky Toki, and White Oak Akashi, then sampled Kaiyō, Kura The Whisky (aged in Japanese rum barrels), YAME Eight Goddesses 10 Year Old, and, later, Nobushi. We sat and talked for hours, trading whisky stories. We went deep into the night.

That weekend Rich and John steeped me in Asian cuisine and, at every chance we got, we scanned the back shelves of bars, looking for Japanese labels we had not yet tasted. It is still a memory we look back on fondly.

JAPANESE WHISKY 101

Japanese whisky can be confusing. "Japan has few rules about what constitutes whiskey, let alone what makes it Japanese. Companies can buy spirits in bulk from abroad, bottle and label it 'Japanese whisky,' and ship it back out," wrote Clay Risen in the *New York Times.* "They can export aged shochu (a distilled spirit) made from grains, like rice or barley, for sale in America as whiskey. Some so-called distilleries don't even do any distilling; they import the whiskey in bulk and contract another company to bottle it." This wasn't really a problem on the world market until Japanese whisky got big. Some of the biggest labels saw the curtain being pulled aside. The industry was embarrassed. Aficionados wanted more transparency. And they got it. In 2021, the definition of "Japanese whisky" was standardized by eighty-two of Japan's companies, with many of the loopholes in Japan's whisky rules closed off. Now all Japanese whisky must contain malted grains (other cereal grains may be included as well). Also, the regulations insist that all production—fermentation to distilling to bottling—must take place in Japan for a product to carry the label "Japanese whisky."

Japanese whisky has long been the domain of collectors. Some stores specialize in Japanese whisky, and have a cadre of customers who pounce on each arrival. Shipments can hit a store one day, and be gone the next. When Japanese whisky got hot, prices began soaring, sometimes doubling, or worse. And scarcity became a problem. Whiskies that were once an obtainable $80 became $160 or even north of $200. Unscrupulous dealers encouraged the highly volatile market. However, things have started to settle.

DRINKING WHISKY IN JAPAN

"The typical Japanese way of drinking whisky, *mizuwari* literally means 'mixed with water.' And it's served during the meal in a glass filled with ice. The whisky is then transformed into a less alcoholic drink which retains most of its flavor," wrote Nicolas Rua of Japanese-Whiskey.com.

"This is the most common way to drink whisky in Japan, especially in Japanese gourmet restaurants." The most popular whisky cocktail in Japan is the Highball: fill a tall glass with large ice cubes, add one shot of whisky, and top off with soda water. It is essentially one part whisky to three parts soda water. That's a great cocktail to last all night long, whether you're having dinner with clients or out with friends.

Suntory Whisky Toki is perfect for such drinks. It is a light whisky, clear gold in color, with a nose of green apple, honey, herbs, and vanilla. The green apple also comes through across the palate, as do herbs and spices, ginger, and honey. Honey and vanilla linger. Toki was modeled on blended Scotch whiskies. It is the perfect Japanese cocktail whisky, and is largely available in America and elsewhere.

According to Stefan Van Eycken, the best Highball in Japan is thought to be served at Rock Fish in Ginza by legendary master Maguchi Kazunari, who makes his with Suntory's Kakubin blended whisky (only available in Asian markets).

NOTABLE EXPRESSIONS

Hibiki

The first time I tasted Hibiki was around 2014. One of our local liquor stores boasted having several bottles. I bought one with the intention of treating myself. I must admit, I had no intention of sharing it with anyone. It was my precious.

Hibiki, which means "resonance," was first developed in 1987 by master blender Keizo Saji to celebrate Suntory's ninetieth anniversary. The chief blender at that time was Koichi Inatomi. Together, the two men tasted thousands of samples, and eventually blended thirty malt whiskies and mellow grain whiskies to come up with the final product. The concept was that the whiskies would come from Suntory's three great distilling sites equally—Yamazaki, Hakushu, and Chita. Each distillery contributed ten malt and grain whiskies. The whiskies were aged in five different cask types. This was considered the best of the best from Suntory.

"It really shows the know-how of Suntory. It's a blend of Scottish base and American influence with Japanese flair. The attention to texture and mouthfeel is incredible, and the way the flavors all meld together is perfect," says Flavien Desoblin, owner of New York City's Brandy Library and Copper & Oak, a bar with a hundred Japanese whiskies.

I bought the Hibiki Japanese Harmony. The elaborate perfume-styled bottle is a jewel in itself. It has twenty-four faceted ridges going up and down the sides of the bottle; in ancient Japan, the year was divided into twenty-four seasons, which is what these ridges represent. It features a Echizen Washi paper label crafted by Eriko Horiki, and the calligraphy is by Tansetsu Ogino. The whisky is amber colored, and on first note is super perfumy in the best possible way. There are floral notes, lychee, herbs, a splash of oak, and hints of sandalwood. But the whisky surprises you, like a delicate Highlands Scotch, with notes of candied orange peel, apple, pear, and a subtle sweetness that lies under the notes on top. It's a combination of the lightest honey and a hint of blossom. Delicate, elegant, complex. Hibiki Japanese Harmony is considered one of the best Japanese whiskies ever produced. The non-age-statement is the easiest to find and is excellent. Other editions are harder to find—Hibiki 12 Year Old, Hibiki 17 Year Old, Hibiki 21 Year Old, and Hibiki 30 Year Old. There's also Hibiki Blossom Harmony, which features whiskies that were combined for the first Hibiki release.

I was overwhelmed at my first reaction to this whisky. I had to tell someone. So, eventually, when Rich came to visit, I shared my bottle with him. I was so seduced by its delicate power, I had to fight against myself to share it. But share it I did because, let's be honest, whisky is only truly good if you are sharing it with someone else.

Try it by itself first, water and whisky back. Then dab a few drops of water in it and let it open up the nose. This is as pretty as whisky gets.

The Yamazaki Single Malt 12 Year Old

"Yamazaki is an area steeped in history. In 1852, it was the site of the famous Battle of Yamazaki. Centuries later, conveniently located between Kyoto and Osaka, it became the birthplace of Japanese whisky," writes Stefan Van Eycken in his book *Whisky Rising*. "At Yamazaki, three rivers—the Katsura, Uji, and Kizu—merge, and because of the differences in water temperature between the three, as well as the topography of the area, mist and fog were common occurrences . . . the area had long been famous for its exquisite water."

The Yamazaki Distillery makes Suntory's flagship single malt whisky. There is nothing colloquial about this distillery. It has eight spirit stills and eight wash stills. The whiskies are made with the best water, and aged in a combination of American, Spanish, and Japanese mizunara oak. Most of the whisky is barreled and then aged 43 miles away at Suntory's Ohmi Aging Cellar near Lake Biwa. This massive warehouse complex was built in 1972, and also includes a cooperage.

The distillery produces, among other whiskies, the famous Yamazaki Single Malt (non-age-statement), Yamazaki 12 Year Old, Yamazaki 18 Year Old, and Yamazaki 25 Year Old. While the non-age-statement is easier to find, the one that most whisky writers covet is the 12 Year Old. It is far more accessible than the other age statements, and more complex than its non-age-statement sibling.

Floral and fruity, this is the granddaddy of them all. It is considered among the best Japanese whiskies produced. "The 12-year-old is the core expression from Yamazaki that Suntory launched way back in 1984," wrote Jonah Flicker for *Esquire* magazine. "The blend of cask types, peated and unpeated whiskies, and even the shape of the stills are what defines Yamazaki."

The current expressions of the whisky are made by fifth-generation chief blender Shinji Fukuyo. Fukuyo has turned back the clock at the same time he is driving it forward, creating deep, complex, and multilayered whiskies that highlight fruit and mizunara notes.

This is a lovely sipping whiskey, complex and well balanced. Yes, you can put in ice and/or water, you heathen. But why?

Nikka Whisky

Masataka Taketsuru was born in Takehara, Hiroshima, in 1894. In 1918, Taketsuru went to Scotland to study distilling and organic chemistry at the University of Glasgow. A year later, he apprenticed at Longmorn Distillery in Strathspey, Scotland, and then another distillery in the Lowlands. He completed one more apprenticeship, then traveled to New York City and Seattle before returning home to Japan with his Scottish-born wife, Jessie, in 1920. Taketsuru worked at Suntory's distillery before going on to found his own, Nikka Whisky, in 1934, in Yoichi on the northern Japanese island of Hokkaido. Taketsuru thought it very much resembled Scotland, including the climate. He originally positioned his operation as an apple drink company, in order to make money while his whisky aged. After many struggles, he released his first whisky in 1940.

Three of my favorites from Nikka are Nikka Yoichi Single Malt, Miyagikyo Single Malt, and Nikka Coffey Single Grain. You can't go wrong with any of them. Yoichi Single Malt is produced at the Yoichi Distillery. Yoichi malts are most often compared to whiskies from Islay, in Scotland. These are bold, strong whiskies that feature notes of peat and smoke, a result of the direct coal-fired distillation.

Miyagikyo Single Malt is produced at Nikka's Miyagikyo Distillery. These whiskies tend to be more like Highland Scotches, elegant and fruity, with a delicate mouthfeel. They feature lightly peated and nonpeated malted barley. Both are lovely. Choose your favorite profile and lean back.

Nikka Coffey Grain Whisky is a unique product, one that should be experienced. The company installed two Coffey stills (named after their inventor, Aeneas Coffey) at the Miyagikyo Distillery in 1999. Coffey stills are not as efficient as column stills, but extract more flavor from the grain, making the resulting whisky bigger and more flavorful. Since it's single grain, it's a predominantly corn mash bill. It's aged three years in re-charred American oak.

The nose starts off with vanilla and nuts, cereal, shortbread, maple syrup, and dried pear and apple. On the palate there's caramel and toast, and notes of toffee, cornbread, and brown sugar. A lovely, light whisky.

Iwai Whisky

The Hombo family first began producing shochu in 1909. The family expanded into whisky in 1949, when it established the Mars Shinshu Distillery. They obtained their license with help from their consultant, Mr. Kiichiro Iwai, an icon in Japanese whisky. Iwai has been called "the Silent Pioneer of Japan Whisky," and was the mentor of Masataka Taketsuru, the founder of Nikka Whisky. It was Iwai who sent Taketsuru to Scotland to study distilling and whisky making.

Today Mars has two distilling sites, the Shinshu and Tsunuki distilleries. Mars Shinshu, the main distillery, was initially located in Kagoshima but in 1984 it was relocated to the Nagano Alps, at an altitude of 2,625 feet. The distillery gets its cold, clear water from the melting glaciers. Mars Tsunuki opened in 2016 in the original Shinshu location. The operation was outfitted with new pot stills, and is Japan's southernmost distillery. They also have a separate aging site on the small island of Yakushima, where they store spirits from both distilleries.

Mars Shinshu makes a number of whiskies, and one of the most popular in the United States is the Iwai family of whiskies. This includes Iwai Mars Whisky, Iwai Tradition (which offers up a series of finishes), Iwai 45, and Iwai Tradition Sherry Cask Finish, all of which are blended whiskies, as well as the Komagatake Single Malt. Among my favorites is the Iwai Mars Whisky in the blue label made with a large amount of corn along with a dose of malt and a hint of rye. The whisky is aged in ex-bourbon barrels. It's a very smooth, clean, delicate bourbon-style whiskey that is super easy to drink. It has hints of sweet corn along with some notes of red fruit, brown sugar, and vanilla. A lovely whisky.

A FEW MORE TO CONSIDER

There are many wonderful whiskies I have left out, including Hakushu 12 Year Old, White Oak Akashi, Mars Maltage "Cosmo," Nikka Whisky From The Barrel, Kikori (a great rice shochu that qualifies as whisky), The Matsui Single Malt Whisky, Fukano Whisky, Chichibu Ichiro's Malt & Grain Limited Edition, Ohishi Whisky Sakura Cask, Shibui Single Grain 18 Year Old, and others. Many are rarities, quickly snatched up by true believers long before you get out of bed.

Next time you're having a steak, and thinking of a bourbon or Scotch, try a Japanese whisky. You will be thrilled you did. Suntory Whisky Toki and Kikori Whisky both go great with sushi. Others pair beautifully with smoked foods. Still others play well with meats or spicy dishes. Or just get a friend and a bottle, and sit back and enjoy. Japanese whiskies are a real treat and the best treats are enjoyed with friends. Share the bottle. It tastes better that way.

WHISKEY COCKTAILS

"When evening quickens in the street, comes a pause in the day's occupation that is known as the cocktail hour. It marks the lifeward turn. The heart wakens from coma and its dyspnea ends," wrote Pulitzer Prize–winning historian Bernard DeVoto in his beautiful ode to sophisticated drinking, *The Hour: A Cocktail Manifesto.* "Its strengthening pulse is to cross over into campground, to believe that the world has not been altogether lost or, if lost, then altogether not in vain."

The word "cocktail" first appeared in rejoinder to a reader's query requesting the word's definition in the May 6, 1806, issue of *The Balance and Columbian Repository* in Hudson, New York. A subsequent response from the editor, a week later, described a blending of spirits, bitters, water, and sugar. It was an early recipe for what would eventually become an Old Fashioned. The spirits then were undefined—rum, whiskey, brandy, etc. Thankfully, there is more artistry about it now.

I love a cocktail at the end of the day. A glass of wine is nice, yes. But a cocktail after the day is done and before the evening meal is a nice way to sit back, relax, and find your own groove again. I fully agree with humorist David Sedaris when he said, "No amount of physical contact could match the healing powers of a well-made cocktail." It is the moment that demarcates the jungle outside and the civilized world within your own walls.

When I was a child, I was lucky enough to spend a lot of time in Connecticut. I grew up in Southport, Westport, Fairfield, and Green during the school year. Those were the last years of the true Connecticut Yankees. Old dyed-in-the-wool types who wore Brooks Brothers and belonged to country clubs, who commuted on trains, reading the *Times* or *Journal* in the morning, and the *Daily News* or *Post* on the way home. Men wore buttoned-down shirts and striped ties. Families had big station wagons, with a third set of seats that looked out the back window, and were sided with faux wood paneling. Everyone went skiing in Vermont in the winter, to Newport or the Cape or the Vineyard in the summer, and spent Christmases traveling. Everyone got the *New Yorker*, *Time*, and *TV Guide*, and at Christmas ordered from B. Altman's or L. L. Bean. You either golfed or played tennis.

We were the last of the children who saw such things. We played all day on our Huffy bikes with banana seats, high handlebars, and three-gear shifters. We played tag on bikes. Our mothers threw us out in the morning. We were allowed to come back for lunch, and were expected home before dark or by five or six for dinner (whichever your family observed).

Not only was I lucky enough to grow up in such a world (at least part of the time), but I was also privileged to live near the family of Bernard and Irene Skomal. Born in the Midwest, Bernie served in the Army, and somehow landed on the East Coast. Irene was born and bred in the Bronx. Bernie was tall and big shouldered, and we called him "the Chief" (when he wasn't around). Irene was an elegant, beautiful woman who moved with grace and dignity and had a mouth like a sailor when you pissed her off (which we did daily).

The Skomals had a very large house, necessary to fit their seven children. It was not the most beautiful house but it had its charm and it was full of life. The neighborhood kids practically lived there. I loved it there. The downstairs had a dining room, sunroom, butler's pantry, a giant kitchen, and an enormous living room. When Bernie came home each night, more often than not Irene greeted him. She usually wore a dress and some earrings. Maybe a little lipstick. And they would convene in the living room where Bernie would decompress and debrief Irene on his day. And Irene would do the same. Sometimes drinks were already made. Sometimes the bar cart awaited whatever they decided on. Martinis were popular. But a highball was always happily accepted.

There were two massive sofas that faced each other in the room. And a chair somewhere in between at one end. Bernie and Irene would sit down and each take a sip. A loosened tie, a sigh. And then they would begin their chat. Children were allowed in the room. We were not allowed to speak. We sat on the opposing sofa, watching the adults like a television set as they sipped their cocktails and spoke.

I marveled at it as if it were theater. My father had no such moment. He came home, changed, came into our kitchen, and we ate. My family seemed more like something out of a Woody Allen film: "Did ya hear, she has cancer!" and other mundane fare. My father, for all his love of cocktails when he was out, never drank anything other than water or weak iced tea with dinner. At that age, like most kids, I couldn't wait to get away from my own parents and experience the world.

I don't ever remember having the fortitude to sit through one of Bernie and Irene's entire conversations, but it was always thrilling to watch the beginning, the ritual of it, and to wonder at it. Their dialogue was convivial, intimate, adult. And I remember thinking, when I grow up, I want to repeat this rite, this crossover from the rough day to the civilized return to the fortress of solitude.

When I grew older, I got into wine first, and often had wine with dinner. And then on weekends I began my own version of this ceremony, wherein I made cocktails while grilling, or in the late afternoon before dinner. It varied, but I found the calming peace of it.

I knew and loved my father, for all his faults, and copied many of his traits, even against my will. I remember how I used to hate when my father would be driving through a neighborhood and see someone he knew. He would pull over and they would begin to chat. My eyes would roll. Seconds turned to hours. It was the same when we went to a restaurant. But when I got older, I also started going to the bar first to have a drink or two, and chat with friends before sitting down to dinner. I became comfortable on a barstool, nursing a cocktail, enjoying the conversation, as my father did.

And that, I think, is the beauty of the cocktail. It's not for swirling. It's not for gulping. It's for sipping. It's for nursing. Because the other side of the cocktail is not just the making, it's the enjoying. The lingering. The conversation. And *that* is what my father was so good at.

Which leads me back to whiskey, and to one of my favorites, Mark Twain. When it comes to whiskey, no one can beat Mark Twain's notion that "too much of anything is bad, but too much whiskey is barely enough."

MARK TWAIN

"Livy, my darling," Twain wrote to his wife from Britain, "I want you to be sure and remember to have, in the bathroom when I arrive, a bottle of Scotch Whiskey, a lemon, some crushed sugar, and a bottle of Angostura bitters. Ever since I have been in London I have taken in a wine glass what is called a cock-tail (made with those ingredients) before breakfast, before dinner, and just before going to bed."

This recipe was Twain's favorite cocktail. It's mostly just a whiskey sour made with Scotch. But it's a fun cocktail to serve to friends. A real conversation starter, and easy to make.

GLASSWARE: Coupe

---

2 oz. / 59 ml blended Scotch whisky

¾ oz. / 22 ml fresh lemon juice

¾ oz. / 22 ml simple syrup

2 dashes of Angostura Bitters

Lemon twist, for garnish

1. Chill the coupe glass by filling it with ice (then dumping it out) or refrigerate it until cold.

2. Blend the Scotch, lemon juice, simple syrup, and bitters in a shaker filled with ice. Shake until cold.

3. Wipe the rim of the glass with the lemon twist.

4. Strain the drink into the chilled coupe glass.

5. Garnish with the twist.

SAZERAC

The topic of what the oldest whiskey cocktail might be has been debated for years. For my money, and in discussing with the experts I know, I believe it probably is the Sazerac. Developed in New Orleans (there is evidence that dates it back to at least 1838), it is one of the most famous cocktails ever. The Sazerac Company trademarked the drink back in 1900, ensuring its place in history.

GLASSWARE: Coupe

Absinthe, to rinse

1 sugar cube

½ teaspoon cold water

4 dashes of Peychaud's bitters

2½ oz. / 74 ml rye whiskey

Lemon twist, for garnish

1. Chill the coupe glass by filling it with ice (then dumping it out) or refrigerate it until cold.

2. Rinse the glass with a bit of absinthe. Dump out any excess.

3. In a separate glass, muddle the sugar cube, water, and bitters.

4. Add the rye and fill the glass with ice. Stir until chilled.

5. Strain the mixture into the chilled coupe glass.

6. Garnish with the lemon twist.

OLD FASHIONED

Again, one of the oldest cocktails. You can use whatever you wish—whiskey, blended Scotch, bourbon, or rye. Some folks will have a heart attack reading that. But it's none of their damned business. Whatever you prefer is best. Over the years, the Old Fashioned has gotten kind of ... well, muddled, for lack of a better word. However, this is the one drink I have a personal problem with. Firstly, since I was introduced to it by Jim Meehan of Please Don't Tell and Robert Simonson of the *New York Times*, I prefer my Old Fashioned with rye. And Dale DeGroff told me to use a better, more potent whiskey so that it stands up to the other ingredients. I like Dad's Hat, at 95 proof, or something similar. I want a pungent whiskey to break through the sweetness. Friend and celebrated cocktail maestro Salvatore Calabrese, among those who brought the classic cocktail scene back in London at Dukes and The Lanesborough hotels, prefers Old Potrero Malted Rye Whiskey, which is also an outstanding choice.

GLASSWARE: Rocks glass

1¼ oz. / 37 ml strong rye whiskey (at least 95 proof)

1½ oz. / 45 ml simple syrup

3 dashes of aromatic bitters

1 strip of orange peel, for garnish

1 cherry, for garnish

1. Combine the rye, simple syrup, and bitters in the rocks glass.

2. Add ice and stir gently until the ice begins to melt and settle.

3. Express the strip of orange peel over the glass.

4. Garnish with the orange peel and cherry.

CHERRIES
An Important Note

Cherries can be a final, sexy touch to a drink. They can also be garish. One needs to be careful, unless you're making a Shirley Temple. There are only a few acceptable brands of cocktail cherries. Luxardo, Fabbri Amarena, Jack Rudy, and Woodford Reserve are preferred. Dark cherries aged in a syrup and/or liquor-based liquid will also do. But I am sorry, maraschino cherries are not allowed in sophisticated cocktails. They are great for sundaes or banana splits but not for any self-respecting cocktail.

FITZ'S OLD FASHIONED

When I was first introduced to the Old Fashioned, I drank it with bourbon. But since my ... let's call it "awakening," I have been blissfully enjoying it with rye.

That was, until I met the renowned mixologist John "Fitz" Fitzpatrick. "Fitz" is a legendary character, raconteur, and one helluva conjurer of magical alcoholic elixirs. He makes, without question, the best bourbon Old Fashioned I have ever had. He serves this incredible cocktail at Warren's American Whiskey Kitchen in Delray Beach, Florida.

GLASSWARE: Rocks glass

Cherrywood chips, as needed

2 oz. / 59 ml Woodford Double Oaked Bourbon

¼ oz. / 7.5 ml simple syrup

2 dashes of orange bitters (Fitz calls them "bangs")

2 dashes of mole (dark chocolate) bitters

Orange twist, for garnish

1. Smoke the rocks glass with cherrywood. There are various ways to do so. Generally, you wet a glass, fire a small mound of cherry or applewood chips/shavings, and set the glass over the chips for a minute.

2. Combine the bourbon, simple syrup, and both bitters in a mixing glass. Add ice and stir.

3. Strain the drink mixture into the smoked rocks glass.

4. Rub the orange twist along the glass rim, then add it to the drink as a garnish.

MANHATTAN

The Manhattan is clocked in many stories. One attributed the cocktail to the Manhattan Club, where it was introduced by Lady Churchill (mother of Winston) to celebrate the candidacy of Samuel J. Tilden. That turned out to be apocryphal. Another story places the date of origin around 1860 at a bar near Houston and Broadway.

The Manhattan at one point was the most ordered cocktail in fine restaurants in America, according to acclaimed whiskey journalist David Wondrich, who conducted an informal poll among his well-placed mixologist friends back in 2013. In fact, the Manhattan became a measuring stick amongst aficionados. "Learn to make a proper Manhattan and you will know how to create at least one flawless thing in this world, and the person you're making it for will know, and respect that about you," Wondrich wrote in *Esquire* magazine.

GLASSWARE: Coupe

---

2 oz. / 59 ml rye (some folks prefer bourbon; they're wrong, but it's their drink)

1 oz. / 29.5 ml sweet vermouth

2 or 3 dashes of Angostura Bitters

Lemon twist, for garnish

Brandied cherry, for garnish (optional)

1. Chill the coupe glass by filling it with ice (then dumping it out) or refrigerate it until cold.

2. Combine the rye, vermouth, and bitters in a shaker.

3. Fill with ice and stir to chill (some like to shake, but the famous mixologists stir).

4. Strain into the chilled coupe glass.

5. Garnish with the lemon twist and, if you like, a brandied cherry.

MINT JULEP

This is the quintessential Kentucky bourbon cocktail. The term "julep" refers generally to a sweet drink that was imbibed back in the day to make medicines go down. The original American mint juleps were mostly medicinal, lightly alcoholic concoctions blended with camphor.

The great popularizer of the drink was U.S. senator Henry Clay of Kentucky, who introduced it to Washington, D.C., at the Round Robin Bar in the famous Willard Hotel in the early half of the nineteenth century. It eventually made its way into the 1862 edition of *Jerry Thomas' Bar-Tenders Guide: How to Mix All Kinds of Plain and Fancy Drinks*.

"I found a mid-nineteenth century julep recipe written as a prescription in an old issue of *Harper's Monthly* and translated it," recalled David Wondrich. "With three parts Cognac, one part rye, and the rest a normal julep, it's a tasty, simple, old-school drink that's good for the summer months. I see it on a lot of cocktail lists now, and it makes me happy."

The Mint Julep cemented its place in history with its being promoted at the Kentucky Derby as long ago as 1938. It is estimated that more than 120,000 juleps are served at Churchill Downs the weekend of the Kentucky Oaks and Kentucky Derby each year.

GLASSWARE: Silver or copper Julep cup

---

6 fresh mint leaves, plus 1 leaf for garnish

½ oz. / 15 ml simple syrup

2 oz. / 59 ml bourbon

1. Combine the mint and simple syrup in the cup. Muddle the leaves gently in the syrup.
2. Add the bourbon.
3. Add crushed ice and stir.
4. Top the cup with more crushed ice.
5. Garnish with a mint leaf.

KENTUCKY MULE

"While spectators in the stands of the Kentucky Derby sip Mint Juleps, tailgaters in the parking lot gather around 'Kentucky Classics,' a cocktail of Ale 8 and bourbon," wrote Mandy Naglich in VinePairs.com.

If the Mint Julep is the grand dame of Kentucky cocktails, her backporch sister is certainly a Kentucky Mule, more commonly known, if you're at a BBQ or a tailgate, as a Bourbon and Ale 8.

Ale 8 (officially named Ale-8-One but known locally as Ale 8) was created by soda bottler G. L. Wainscott in 1926. Allegedly it was originally called "A Late One" and eventually morphed into "Ale-8-One." It is generally thought to be a blend of ginger ale and citrus flavors and is an iconic southern brand. Until 2001 it was only available in Kentucky but can now be found throughout the southern United States and lower Midwest. If you can't find it in your area, ginger ale is an amiable substitute. Perhaps add an extra lime wedge.

GLASSWARE: Rocks glass or highball glass

---

2 oz. / 59 ml bourbon

4 oz. / 118 ml Ale 8

Lime wedge, for garnish

1. Fill the glass with crushed ice.

2. Pour the bourbon over the ice.

3. Add the Ale 8 and the lime wedge.

4. Stir gently.

VARIATIONS: There are a slew of iterations of this classic drink. Some folks like to add a bit of simple syrup or 2 ounces of grenadine. Others include bitters such as orange Angostura. Still others will add 1 ounce each of lime juice and Triple Sec. I have also seen a version that includes 1 oz. fresh lemon juice and a crushed or sliced up strawberry.

RUSTY NAIL

"For decades, one of the hottest cocktails was the Rusty Nail. But after a good run, the simple combination of scotch and the scotch-based liqueur Drambuie, a word derived from Gaelic meaning 'the drink that satisfies,' has fallen off most bar menus and is rarely ordered by patrons," wrote Dale DeGroff in 2020.

The drink has a quirky past. There was a very similar libation that was popular in London in the late 1930s. It first appeared in print in the *Old Mr. Boston Official Bartender's Guide* in 1967. The drink may have come from the clever staff at the 21 Club.

"Lore has it that the Rat Pack was enamored with the drink, which may have been responsible for the wide appeal in those years," according to De-Groff. "In the 1970s, I mixed many a Rusty Nail at the joints I worked at in New York. They were also a hit at P.J. Clarke's, a favorite late-night haunt of Frank Sinatra."

That makes sense to me because there was a time when it was always important that we had Benedictine and Drambuie in the house, both big mixers when I was a kid. Sinatra was famous for loving a Jack Daniel's Rusty Nail, a variation, since it was supposed to be made with Scotch.

GLASSWARE: Rocks glass

1½ oz. / 44.5 ml Scotch whisky

¾ oz. / 22 ml Drambuie

Lemon twist, for garnish

1. Fill a mixing glass with ice.
2. Add the Scotch and Drambuie and stir until chilled.
3. Place one large ice cube in the rocks glass.
4. Strain the mixture into the glass.
5. Garnish with the lemon twist.

A Dusty Rusty Nail

My mom and stepfather live in the backcountry of Connecticut, and are ardent tag sale and estate sale searchers; they both have an excellent eye for antique shop–worthy items. One Christmas I was handed a wrapped present. For sure it was liquor. I unwrapped it carefully only to find an ancient bottle of Drambuie still in its original box, obviously generations old. My parents had found it at an estate sale. The seal was still unbroken. They had bought it for five dollars as a gag, thinking it humorous.

It sat in my wine cellar for another ten years before I gave it a second glance. It wasn't until I read about the boom in "dusty hunters" that I entertained the idea of cracking the seal. "Dusty bottles" were old, unopened bottles of whiskey, and people who searched for them were called "dusty hunters." I prepared for a side-by-side taste test: new versus old.

The current version of Drambuie is a gorgeous golden color, with a big floral nose and immense amounts of fresh, golden heather honey, anise, and clove. A big, bright, and lovely dram. It's the number one selling Highlands liqueur in the world—and it is very good!

The bottle my parents found was likely released in the late 1950s or early 1960s, which I sussed out from the liquor seal and by looking at advertisements from the period. The older Drambuie is an amber color, and has a softer nose with a nuttiness not present in the newer bottle, and a hint of sherry. There's nice spice on the nose as well. The anise and clove are more integrated, subtler, and there is a slight, light smokiness to the nose. An absolutely exquisite dram.

Then I found another dusty, 35-year-old bottle of 15-year-old Pinch Scotch. Putting two and two together, I made one morning, at 8:30 a.m., at my local coffee shop (which doubled as a bar at night) six Dusty Rusty Nails that were approximately 50 years old! Among those who partook was the legendary award-winning composer, producer, and engineer, Scott Petito. A once-in-a-lifetime treat. Anytime I see one of those guys, they always bring it up. A very special memory.

ROB ROY

My father's favorite drink, the Rob Roy, was invented in 1894 by a bartender at the Waldorf-Astoria in New York City to coincide with the premiere of *Rob Roy*, an operetta about Scottish folk hero Rob Roy MacGregor. It is made in the same style as a Manhattan but with Scotch whisky.

GLASSWARE: Coupe

---

2 oz. / 59 ml Scotch whisky

¾ oz. / 22 ml sweet vermouth

3 dashes of Angostura Bitters

Brandied cherry, for garnish

1. Fill a mixing glass with ice.
2. Add the Scotch, vermouth, and bitters and stir until chilled.
3. Strain into the coupe.
4. Garnish with the cherry.

BOULEVARDIER

A boulevardier is a man-about-town. The cocktail took its name from a 1920s Parisian magazine of the same name, published by American writer Erskine Gwynne. The cocktail was memorialized in Harry MacElhone's 1927 book, *Barflies and Cocktails.* It was an overnight sensation, and has since gone on to be a solid fixture in the whiskey cocktail universe.

The most memorable Boulevardier I have ever had was served to me by mixologist Darren Joseph at the Deer Mountain Inn, in Tannersville, New York. A former mansion turned sophisticated inn, the Deer Mountain Inn has a small mahogany bar that is flanked by two huge Adirondack camp—style stone fireplaces, and lots of Persian carpets and leather chairs. Darren's Boulevardier is legendary. And I insisted that every person I brought to the inn after that try it, including my legendary East Coast tasting teammate Rich Srsich and Emmy Award—winning writer Jo Miller. I've closed the bar with Darren several times. His Christopher Walken imitation is spot on.

GLASSWARE: Rocks glass

1¼ oz. / 37 ml bourbon or rye

1 oz. / 29.5 ml Campari

1 oz. / 29.5 ml sweet vermouth

Orange twist, for garnish

1. Fill a mixing glass with ice.

2. Add the bourbon, Campari, and vermouth. Stir until chilled.

3. Add ice to the rocks glass (preferably one large cube, if possible).

4. Strain the drink into the rocks glass.

5. Wipe the rim of the glass with the orange twist, then add to the drink as garnish.

BROOKLYN

The Brooklyn is similar to a Manhattan, but is very strict about its bitters, and has the addition of maraschino liqueur. The Brooklyn first appeared in a cocktail book around 1908, and then again in 1913. It was popular for a decade, before it disappeared during Prohibition. It made a big comeback in the 2000s when whiskey started to make a comeback. It calls for Amer Picon or Bigallet China-China Amer for a truly authentic Brooklyn, but two dashes of Angostura bitters will suffice as an acceptable substitute.

GLASSWARE: Coupe

---

2 oz. / 59 ml rye whiskey

1 oz. / 29.5 ml dry vermouth

¼ oz. / 7.5 ml maraschino liqueur

¼ oz. / 7.5 ml Amer Picon (or whatever substitute)

3 brandied cherries, for garnish

1. Chill the coupe by filling it with ice (then dumping it out) or refrigerate it until cold.

2. Fill a mixing glass with ice to the brim.

3. Add the rye, vermouth, maraschino liqueur, and bitters and stir until chilled.

4. Strain into the chilled coupe.

5. Top with the brandied cherries on a cocktail pick.

WHISKEY SOUR

I love Rich Srsich, my sarcastic traveling companion, but there was a night I cursed him out. We went to the Deer Mountain Inn to see Darren Joseph. It was a Saturday, and I knew the bar would be packed. Rich had mentioned that he was really jonesing for a Whiskey Sour. And I admonished him, saying that Darren wouldn't be using any kind of mix. And if the bar was packed, why not give Darren a break, and not order one. Whiskey sours are fun to make when you're not beholden to twenty other people. But in a packed restaurant/bar it was another story. Rich nodded.

Salvatore Calabrese, whom I am lucky enough to know, calls the Whiskey Sour the King of All Sours. He points out that the first sour drink with lemons was made with brandy in Europe. But the Whiskey Sour soon overtook it. It appears in the original edition of *Jerry Thomas' Bar-Tender's Guide*, which dates it back to 1862.

The first sour recipes did not use egg whites. Famed mixologist Gary "Gaz" Regan did not use an egg white in his version, nor does David Wondrich; however, Salvatore, Dale DeGroff, and Canadian mixologist/rock star Dave Mitton all do. More often than not mixologists use an egg white to get a lovely frothy experience.

Many bars use bourbon but others use a blended whiskey, or insist on Scotch (in this last instance you now have a Scotch Sour). It really is up to personal preference. Whiskies like Jack Daniel's, Maker's Mark, Jim Beam, Wild Turkey, Crown Royal, Seagram's 7 Crown, Dewar's, and many others are great choices for this drink. Some people prefer rye for a spicier flavor, while others like the smokiness of a Scotch blend. DeGroff uses a high-strength bourbon.

Darren greeted us enthusiastically when we walked into a bar three people deep. We waited patiently. Then Darren asked us for our drink orders. I got the Boulevardier. Rich hesitated. Darren sensed something, which, of course, is why he was so great. Darren said with a smile, "Tell me what you want."

"Carlo told me not to order it," laughed Rich. Darren enthusiastically demanded to know what it was.

"A Whiskey Sour," admitted Rich.

"Done," said Darren. I rolled my eyes. In the middle of the dinner/bar rush Darren stopped everything and put on a show. He pulled out a fresh egg and separated it with a showman's flair, and, like a magician, served up one of the frothiest Whiskey Sours I have ever seen. Two problems immediately arose. There was a pileup of orders for the dining room and at least five other patrons, after watching the show, asked for a Whiskey Sour.

"You better make sure you drop an extra twenty on Darren," I said. "You just made this guy's life hell for the next 45 minutes." Rich was over the moon. I was buying. He was tipping. And Rich said it was the best Whiskey Sour he ever had.

GLASSWARE: Rocks glass

1 egg white

1½ oz. / 44.5 ml whiskey of choice

¾ oz. / 22 ml simple syrup

½ oz. / 15 ml fresh lemon juice

Lemon twise, for garnish

Brandied cherry (optional), for garnish

1. Fill a shaker with ice.

2. Add the egg white, whiskey, simple syrup, and lemon juice and shake until frothy and chilled.

3. Fill the rocks glass with ice and strain the drink into it.

4. Garnish with the lemon twist and/or brandied cherry (if desired).

WHISKEY SMASH

This cocktail dates back to the 1887 edition of Jerry Thomas's classic bartending book (it went by several names over its different editions). It is definitely a cousin of the Whiskey Sour and very well may be the forerunner to it. It is simpler and has no lasting froth.

GLASSWARE: Tumbler or rocks glass

---

5 to 6 large fresh mint leaves, or to taste

¼ lemon, sliced into 2 or 3 wedges

2 oz. / 59 ml whiskey (usually bourbon, but drinker's choice)

1 oz. / 29.5 ml simple syrup

1. Add 3 or 4 of the mint leaves to a shaker and muddle gently.

2. Add the lemon wedges and muddle again.

3. Add the whiskey and simple syrup.

4. Fill the shaker with ice and shake until chilled.

5. Strain into the tumbler and top with crushed ice.

6. Garnish with the remaining 2 mint leaves.

WHISKEY & SODA

"The biggest trend is the highball, which is basically a whiskey soda. We're seeing it more with Japanese and Scotch whisky," said Jim Meehan in 2018. "As people become more aware of sugar and overconsumption, drinking a highball is basically like drinking a glass of water with each whiskey. It also doesn't add powerful new flavors like a cocktail would—it just dilutes the concentration." Experienced whiskey drinkers tend to agree. Whiske & Soda is the most popular cocktail in Japan.

Whiskey & Soda is light, refreshing, easy to drink and nurse, and you can have a few without really getting toasty. It's a great hot weather whiskey drink. Especially in summer, I prefer to use a lighter-style blended whiskey with a lower alcohol setting, like 80 proof.

GLASSWARE: Collins glass

1½ oz. / 44.5 ml whiskey

4½ oz. / 133 ml premium soda water

Grapefruit or lemon slice (some prefer a twist), for garnish

1. Fill the Collins glass with ice cubes.

2. Add the whiskey and stir.

3. Add the soda and gently stir to just mix.

4. Wipe the rim of the glass with the grapefruit or lemon slice, then garnish the drink with it.

HIGHBALL

My understanding is that the Highball was traditionally made with ginger ale. That's old-school stuff, dating back to the 1950s and 1960s. As a child, I often served as bartender to my father's friends during the summer. Sitting in aluminum folding chairs, wearing their sunglasses, they were Highball drinkers. The idea was to keep them light, so they had something to sip all afternoon. They talked sports and news, and made fun of each other. I loved listening to them when I wasn't in the pool myself. I tried to man my station because if I was there long enough, one of my father's friends would hand me five dollars as a tip for the day. If I was lucky, and they didn't know, I collected $10 between them. I thought it was great fun either way.

Classic blended Scotch and ginger ale with a slice of lemon or lime. The beauty of it is you can use Canadian whisky, Irish whiskey, blended Scotch, bourbon, whatever you like.

Fancier versions exist. The usual 2 ounces of whiskey is pared back to 1½ ounces, and a half ounce of an additional liqueur is added. Sometimes a different soda is used, like a more expressive ginger ale, or ginger beer, another soda, or, even more exotic, a light sparkling wine. Some folks like to add a cherry. Have at it. I prefer a classic Highball, as I have known them. Popular variations include the Seven & Seven, where 7UP stands in for the ginger ale, and a Rye & Coke, where rye whiskey and Coca-Cola are combined.

GLASSWARE: Collins glass

---

2 oz. whiskey

4 oz. ginger ale, chilled

Lemon or lime slice, for garnish

1. Fill the Collins glass with ice cubes.

2. Add the whiskey.

3. Add the chilled ginger ale.

4. Wipe the rim with the lemon or lime slice, then use it to garnish the drink.

ACKNOWLEDGMENTS

No one is self-taught. That's a silly idea. At one point you obtain information from someone or somewhere. I am lucky, beyond all measure. When it comes to wine, beer, and spirits, I have truly sat on the shoulders of giants. I have had the privilege of having published, edited, or worked with such authors as Michael Jackson, Gary Regan, Salvatore Calabrese, Clay Risen, Jim Meehan, Stefan Van Eycken, Lew Bryson, Amanda Schuster, Amy Zavatto, Kurt Maitland, Richard Thomas, Dave Wondrich, Chip Tate, Davin DeKergommeaux, Dave Mitton, Christine Sismondo, Stephen Beaumont, and many others.

Any author of such an effort owes a great debt of gratitude to those who went before him. During the course of my research, I pored over numerous sources, including interviews and articles, from various websites, blogs, newspapers, magazines, and scholarly journals. Special thanks and appreciation for their constant beat coverage (news stories, reviews, and books) of the whiskey industry go to Chuck Cowdery, Michael Veach, Fred Minnick, Nino Marchetti, Eric Burke, Steve Akley, Brett Atlas, Carla Harris Carlton, Susan Reigler, Maggie Kimberl, Josh Peters, and many, many others.

Also important were those who are part of my New England Craft Beverage Research Team, including Rich Srsich, John Crabtree, and Dan Kirkhus. In numerous odd combinations, they were fellow drivers, tasters, and opinion makers. Their friendship and time are much appreciated. I spent many hours on the road, especially with Srsich and Crabtree. Kirkhus and I have spent countless hours tasting through a pallet's worth of whiskey.

I also owe a debt of gratitude to Buz Teacher, one of the founders of Running Press, who introduced me to the world of fine spirits and wines, when we started doing "sin" books back in the 1990s, featuring cigars, wines, whiskies, and other gourmet food titles. He introduced me to Michael Jackson, Gary Regan, and many others.

I would, of course, like to thank John Whalen (*père et fils*) of Cider Mill Press Book Publishers, who helped make this book a reality. Were it not for their excitement, enthusiasm, and faith in me, this book would not have happened. I also owe a huge debt of gratitude to Cider Mill staffers Buzz Poole and Steve Cooley, and editor Pam Kingsley, who helped mold a rather large, unwieldy mess of a manuscript into readable shape in record time.

Finally, thank you to the countless publicity, marketing, sales, and tasting room individuals who helped me and put up with my endless questions and harassment. Thank you.

ABOUT THE AUTHOR

Carlo DeVito is one of the most experienced wine, beers, and spirits editors in the world, whose list of authors has included *The Wine Spectator*, *The New York Times*, Michael Jackson, Kevin Zraly, Clay Risen, Matt Kramer, Oz Clarke, Tom Stevenson, Howard G. Goldberg, Josh M. Bernstein, Stephen Beaumont, Ben McFarland, Jim Meehan, Salvatore Calabrase, William Dowd, and many others.

His books and authors over the years have won James Beard, Gourmand, and IAACP awards. He has traveled to wine regions in California, Canada, up and down the east coast, France, Spain, and Chile. He is the author of more than 20 books, including *Big Whiskey*, *Tennessee Whiskey*, and the *Spirit of Rye*.

ABOUT CIDER MILL PRESS
BOOK PUBLISHERS

Good ideas ripen with time. From seed to harvest, Cider Mill Press brings
fine reading, information, and entertainment together between the covers of its
creatively crafted books. Our Cider Mill bears fruit twice a year,
publishing a new crop of titles each spring and fall.

"Where Good Books Are Ready for Press"
501 Nelson Place
Nashville, Tennessee 37214

cidermillpress.com